SCHOPENHAUER'S EARLY *FOURFOLD ROOT*

T0299961

To Jan

F.C. WHITE

LONDON AND NEW YORK

Notice:
Product or corporate names may be trad
are used only for identification and exp

British Library Cataloguing in Pub

White, F. C.
    Schopenhauer's early *fourfold*
    commentary
    1.Schopenhauer, Arthur, 1788-
    I.Title
    193

Library of Congress Catalog Card

ISBN 13: 978-1-138-27685-7 (pbk)
ISBN 13: 978-1-85972-656-3 (hbk)

Contents

Acknowledgements

For scrutiny of the text and comment I wish to thank Dr Moira Nicholls, Mr John Nerhmann and Mr Christopher Riley; and for editorial guidance the staff of Avebury.

Preface

Schopenhauer was born in Danzig in 1788, the year before the French Revolution began, and spent most of his early years in Hamburg. His formal education was not systematic, but he learned a great deal from his travels and from living abroad, and already in his teens he spoke and read French and English as well as his native German. For some time, under the influence of his father's wishes, he intended to devote his life to the family business, but shortly after his father's death in 1805 he left Hamburg to pursue his education. In 1809, at the age of 21, he matriculated and started his studies at the University of Göttingen, and in 1811 moved to the University of Berlin, where Fichte was lecturing. Two years later, to escape the upheavals of war, he withdrew to the small town of Rudolstadt, where he spent several months writing a doctoral thesis, *On the Fourfold Root of the Principle of Sufficient Reason*, submitting it to the University of Jena. The thesis earned him his doctorate, and at the end of 1813 he paid to have it published — having made some alterations and additions. Shortly afterwards he went to Dresden, where he spent the next four years writing his major work, *The World as Will and Representation*, which was published in December 1818. In 1847 Schopenhauer brought out a second edition of the *Fourfold Root*, more than thirty years after its initial appearance, revising much of what he had written in 1813 and adding to it so extensively that the result was in many respects a quite different book.

No English translation of the edition of 1813 has been published before, so that students unfamiliar with German have had difficulty in appreciating the development of Schopenhauer's thought. They tend to assume that the widely translated *Fourfold Root* of 1847 is in substance the same as that of 1813, and this assumption is encouraged by Schopenhauer's own assertions that his thought did not change radically over the years. But it did. At any rate it underwent radical development. To illustrate the point, most of what is said in the second edition of the *Fourfold Root* concerning the nature of perception and its relation to the world of everyday experience is not even foreshadowed in the first edition. It is clear, then, that if we wish to know what Schopenhauer in 1818 considered necessary to an adequate understanding of *The World as Will and Representation*, we must read the first edition of the *Fourfold Root*, not the edition of 1847. More generally, if we wish to acquire a good understanding of the development of Schopenhauer's thought, we must be familiar with both editions of the *Fourfold Root*.

In many respects the edition of 1813 is a brilliant work. With daring economy it attempts in fewer than a hundred pages to establish what are the ultimate metaphysical components of phenomenal reality and the principles of explanation governing them. However, in spite of its brilliance and the underlying simplicity of its aim and execution, for many reasons Schopenhauer's treatise is not easy to read. It assumes acquaintance with the works of other philosophers, particularly the works of Kant; it makes far reaching philosophical assumptions in almost every section; it puts forward arguments and criticisms that are often sketchy and leave the reader guessing how they are to be filled out; it lacks examples at crucial points; it introduces discussions within the main body of the text that would better have been left to appendices; above all, it is too short for a sustained development of any of its major themes. Consequently, the *Fourfold Root* is a work that many scholars will read several times before feeling confident of having understood it, and beginners are likely to experience difficulty in discerning even its main tenets and arguments. For these reasons, I have added a fairly detailed survey with comments after Chapter Eight of Schopenhauer's text.

1 Introduction

§1 The method

The divine Plato and truly remarkable Kant unite their voices in emphatically recommending a rule of method for the pursuit of all philosophy, indeed for the pursuit of all knowledge.[1] There are two laws, they say, that should be complied with equally, the law of *homogeneity* and the law of *specification*, neither being made use of to the disadvantage of the other.

The *law of homogeneity* enjoins that we take note of similarities and conformities, that in the light of this we group things under species and species under genera, that we place lower genera under higher, and that we continue in this way until we arrive at a unity of a highest, all-embracing kind.

Since the law of homogeneity is transcendental and therefore essential to our reason, it presupposes nature to be in conformity with it, and this presupposition is expressed in the ancient principle, *Entities are not to be multiplied beyond necessity.*[2] The *law of specification* on the other hand, as expressed by Kant, is as follows: *The number of varieties of things is not to be reduced without serious consideration.*[3] This second law requires us to distinguish clearly the various genera united under a comprehensive general notion, and again the higher and lower species under these genera, without at any point making a leap. In particular it requires us not to subsume lowest-level species, let alone concrete individuals, immediately under the general notion, since all concepts are capable of further subdivision, none reaching down to the level of bare perception.

According to Kant, both laws are transcendental a priori principles of reason, postulating conformity between things and themselves, and Plato in his own way seems to say the same: he asserts that these rules, to which all the sciences owe their origin, were cast down to us from the abode of the gods together with Promethean fire.

§2 Application of the method in the present case

Notwithstanding such an emphatic recommendation, I find that the second of these laws has not been sufficiently applied to the basic principle of knowledge known as the *principle of sufficient reason*. For, although philosophers have frequently and for a long time formulated this principle in general terms, they have neglected properly to distinguish its fundamentally different applications. They have not ascribed to each a different meaning, and consequently have not revealed the source of each in a different constitutive power of the mind.

Particularly in considering the powers of the mind, applying the principle of homogeneity while neglecting its opposite has engendered a host of enduring errors. By contrast, the application of the principle of specification has produced great and significant advances, as is clear from a comparison between Kant and earlier philosophers. Let me therefore quote a passage from Kant recommending the application of the principle of specification to the sources of our knowledge, a passage that consequently favours my present endeavours.

It is most important to isolate kinds of knowledge that are distinct in species and origin, taking care not to run them together after the fashion of ordinary usage. What the chemist does in the analysis of substances and what the mathematician does in the pure study of quantity is even more incumbent upon the philosopher. It enables him to determine with certainty the part played by any given form of knowledge in the diverse uses of the understanding, and to determine the special value and influence of each such form of knowledge. (*CPR*, B870.)

§3 An advantage that this inquiry could bring

If I succeed in showing that the principle constituting the subject matter of this inquiry does not derive immediately from a *unique* form of the intellect's cognition but in the first instance from *several*, it will follow that the necessity that accompanies it in virtue of its being an unalterable a priori principle will not be unique either. It will be as multiple as the sources of the principle. If this is so, however, those who base conclusions upon the principle have the obligation of specifying precisely which of the forms of necessity arising from it they are appealing to. They have the further obligation of giving special names to those forms, following the lead that I shall myself give in making various suggestions.

It is to be hoped that in this way something will be done towards increasing clarity and precision in philosophy, since the highest level of comprehension attained through precise definitions of meanings is essential to philosophy. It preserves us from both error and intentional deceit, and it secures all forms of knowledge gained through philosophy in safe possession, not to be snatched from it as the result of some subsequently discovered misunderstanding or ambiguity. Horace's fable of the country mouse and city mouse has application here, since in philosophy we should prefer a little held in confidence and with unshakeable certainty to a lot based for the most part on rhetoric. For rhetoric is merely concerned with making assertions and being impressive, and may therefore be upset at any moment by honest and courageous criticism.

It seems to me that anything likely to foster better communication should be welcome to philosophers, especially given that complaints are frequently heard from them that they are not understood, and complaints from their readers that they are obscure; yet doubtless both parties wish to make themselves properly understood. Or could there perhaps be periods in history in which intelligibility and the understanding accompanying it are dreaded and shunned? If there are, such times may well be happy in themselves; they may even be religious and virtuous. But they will never be philosophical. For the aim of philosophy is lucidity and clarity. Philosophers endeavour to resemble, not a troubled and turbid stream, but a lake in Switzerland, tranquilly possessing depth together with a clarity that renders that depth visible. Furthermore, I believe that if a person possesses the rare quality of thoroughly understanding himself, he will be able to make himself understood by others, provided that these in turn possess the correspondingly rare quality of wanting to understand. For all men possess both the abilities and the basic truths needed for understanding, even if the degree to which they possess them is not the same in all. Indeed there are few that possess them to an eminent degree, which explains why so few are capable of productions in the arts or discoveries and inventions in the sciences. By contrast, all of us have the ability to some extent to receive, understand and recognise what is correct, so long as it is presented to us clearly — that is, unencumbered by side issues. For this reason, a person who creates something out of his own powers is like a musical instrument, while the rest of us are like receptacles of glass or metal. For while these latter do not themselves produce music, they do echo and propagate the sounds of the instrument.

It must be added, however, that only pure sounds are echoed back, never impure sounds, and that this fact causes frustration in many. It may even explain why the didactic tone in certain writings so often gives way to one of scolding, readers being taken to task in advance and in anticipation of their lack of ability.

§4 Importance of the principle of sufficient reason

The principle of sufficient reason is so important that I have no hesitation in calling it the basis of all science. For *science* is organised knowledge, a system of interconnected items of knowledge; not a bare aggregate. What then is it that holds the parts of such a system together? It is the principle of sufficient reason. For the thing that distinguishes a science from a bare aggregate is precisely that its component truths follow from others as their grounds. Moreover, most sciences contain truths about causes from which effects may be determined, and likewise other truths about the necessity with which conclusions follow from reasons, as will appear in the course of this investigation.

The supposition constantly made by us a priori that all things have a reason is precisely what justifies our asking *why* at every turn, and because of this we may call such a *why* the mother of all sciences.

3

§5 The principle itself

It will become clear later on that the principle of sufficient reason is a common expression for several truths given to us a priori, but since the principle must be given some sort of provisional formulation in the meantime, I choose that of Wolff as being the widest in scope: *Nothing is without a reason why it is rather than not.*[4]

Notes

1   Platon, Phileb. pp. 219-223, edit. Bip; Kant, Kritik d. reinen Vern., pp. 673-688, 2te u. folgende Ausg. (The edition of Plato referred to by Schopenhauer is the edition published at Bipontium 1781-87; the passage of the Philebus referred to is roughly 16c-18d in Stephanus pagination (FW).)
2   Entia praeter necessitatem non esse multiplicanda.
3   Entium varietates non temere esse minuendas.
4   Nihil est sine ratione cur potius sit quam non sit.

2 A survey of the principal doctrines put forward so far concerning the principle of sufficient reason

§6 A first statement of the principle and a distinction between two of its applications

Because the principle of sufficient reason is fundamental to all knowledge, some abstract and more or less adequately defined expression of it was doubtless formulated very early on, and for this very reason it could be difficult to establish where the first expression of it occurs. It is of no great interest anyway.

Plato and Aristotle give no formal expression to it as a major fundamental principle, but they do often speak of it as being self-evident. Plato, with a naivete which, against the background of the critical analysis of recent times, appears like the original state of innocence compared with the knowledge of good and evil, says the following. 'Whatever comes into being has to come into being through a cause. How could it come into being without one?'[1] Aristotle, in his *Posterior Analytics*, I, 2, expresses the principle after a fashion in the following words. 'We think that we fully understand something when concerning its cause we believe that in fact it is its cause, and that there is no other possibility.'[2] Also, already in his *Metaphysics*, IV, 1, he presents a division of various kinds of reason, or rather various kinds of principle, ἀρχαί, of which he assumes there to be eight; although his division is neither thorough nor sufficiently precise. None the less, what he says is quite correct: 'All principles have this in common, that they are the first things through which anything exists, comes into being, or is known.'[3] And in the following chapter he distinguishes various kinds of cause, although again rather

5

arbitrarily. However, he does better in the *Posterior Analytics*, II, 11, where he states that there are four kinds of reason. 'There are four kinds of reason: a thing's essence, its necessitating conditions, that which first put it in motion, and its purpose.'[4]

The principle that nothing is without a cause was an axiom for the scholastics too; though according to Wolff Leibniz was the first to state it formally and to give it general expression. Leibniz was also the first clearly to distinguish two applications of it. He distinguished an application to judgments, stating that for any judgment to be true it must have a ground from which it follows, and an application to changes in the external world, stating that such changes cannot occur without a cause.

§7 Descartes

Even in the works of the astute Descartes we find no clear understanding of this distinction. In his Reply to the Second Set of Objections to *Meditations on First Philosophy*, Axiom 1, he writes as follows. 'Concerning anything that exists it is possible to ask what is the cause of its existing. This question may even be asked concerning God; not because God needs a cause in order to exist, but because the immensity of His nature is the cause or reason why He does not need a cause in order to exist.'[5] What Descartes ought to have written is, 'God's immensity is the rational ground from which it follows that God has no need of a cause.' But he confounds the two relevant forms of the principle, and from this it is plain that he has no clear awareness of the vast difference between cause and rational ground.

§8 Spinoza

Spinoza likewise has no clear grasp of the difference between ground and consequent on the one hand and cause and effect on the other. This is plain from countless passages of his writings, though I shall limit myself to a few examples. In his *Ethics*, Part. III, Prop. 1, Proof, he says: 'From any given *idea* some effect must follow of necessity.'[6] And his Proposition 4 goes as follows. 'Nothing can be destroyed except by a cause external to it. *Proof*: The *definition* of anything affirms and does not deny the essence (essence, nature, as distinct from *existentia*, existence) of that thing; that is, it postulates the essence of the thing and does not negate it. It follows that so long as we attend to the thing itself and not to external causes, we shall not be able to discover anything in it that could destroy it.'[7]

What this amounts to saying is that since a concept can contain nothing contradictory to its definition — that is, the sum of its predicates — a thing likewise can contain nothing that could become the cause of its destruction. Total confusion is evident here between reason and consequent on the one hand and cause and effect on the other. Many other examples of the sort are to be found in the *Ethics*: e.g., Part I, Def. 1; Prop. 11, Proof 2; Prop. 24, Coroll.; Prop. 28, Proof and Scholion.

Not only are these and like cases to be found, but the mistaking and confusing of the two relations is completely entwined at the very foundation of Spinoza's system. (Of course what concerns us here is only the demonstrative part, the part concerned with proof.) He posits a substance, God, with thought and extension as attributes or accidents. But substance and accident existing in external reality are correlative to subject and predicate in judgments. Therefore, given that in analytic judgments all predicates follow from the concept of the subject, the same relation must hold between substance and accident as holds between rational ground and consequent, and Spinoza accordingly assumes that it holds between God and the world. 'From the necessity of the divine nature everything must follow that comes under the heading of infinite intellect.'[8] (*Ethics*, Part I, Prop. 16.) At the same time, throughout his work he refers to God as the cause of the world. 'Whatever exists expresses the power of God, which is the *cause* of everything.'[9] (Ibid., Prop. 36.) 'God is the immanent but not the transient *cause* of everything.' (Ibid., Prop. 18.) 'God is the *efficient cause* not only of the existence of things but of their essence.'[10] (Ibid., Prop. 25.) The above cited passages furnish plenty of examples.

In short, total confusion of the concepts of rational ground and consequent with those of cause and effect lies at the very heart of Spinoza's exposition.

§9 Leibniz

Leibniz then is the first philosopher in whose writings we discover a clear grasp of the distinction in question. In his *Principles of Philosophy* he makes a definite distinction between rational ground (*ratio cognoscendi*) and efficient cause (*causa efficiens*), and he puts these forward as two applications of the principle of sufficient reason (*principium rationis sufficientis*), formally stating this as one of the main principles of knowledge.

§10 Wolff

Wolff introduces the principle of sufficient reason not within logic, as is done nowadays, but within ontology. In that context (*Ontology*, §71) he urges us indeed not to confuse the principle of sufficient rational ground with that of cause and effect, but does not clearly characterise the distinction at issue and is guilty of confusion himself in the very chapter at issue — 'On the Principle of Sufficient Reason.'(§§70, 74, 75, 77.) Here, in support of the principle of sufficient reason, he cites many examples of cause and effect, motive and action; but, had he wished to keep to his distinction, he ought to have cited these in his chapter, 'On Causes,' of the same work. In this chapter, he cites similar examples and again introduces the notion of rational ground (§876), but this clearly does not belong here and has been dealt with elsewhere. Further, he says that, 'by a principle is meant that which contains within itself the reason for something else,'[11] and he goes on to distinguish three such principles.

1. The principle of becoming (*principium fiendi* (*causa*)). This he defines as 'the reason of the actuality of something else (*ratio actualitatis alterius*),' and by way of illustration he says that if a stone grows hot, it is fire or the rays of the sun that constitute the reason for the heat in the stone.[12]

2. The principle of being (*principium essendi*). This he defines as 'the reason of the possibility of something else (*ratio possibilitatis alterius*).' Making use of the example of the stone, he says that the reason for the possibility of a stone's being able to absorb heat lies in the essence or mode of composition of the stone.[13] This seems an altogether empty concept, allowing of nothing to be thought through it. For, as Kant has clearly enough shown, possibility is correspondence with the conditions of all experience, and these are known to us a priori. From them we know, to take Wolff's example of the stone, that changes in it are possible as effects: that is, we know that one state can follow another if the first contains the conditions of the second. Thus the state of the stone's being hot is the effect, its cause being the preceding state of a finite capacity for heat in the stone and its contact with free heat. Why Wolff wishes to call the first of these two components of the causal state the heat's principle of being (*principium essendi*), the second its principle of becoming (*principium fiendi*), I do not understand. The stone is such as it is, with such and such a capacity for heat and so on, and this fact is the consequence of a series of earlier causes, of principles of becoming (*principiorum fiendi*), just as is the stone's contact with free heat. The conjoining of the two components constitutes that state of affairs which, as cause, produces the stone's being hot as effect. There is consequently no place for Wolff's 'principle of being,' and I do not acknowledge there to be any such thing. My only reason for making so lengthy a mention of it is that I use the expression myself later on, though in a very different sense.

3. As I have already pointed out, Wolff distinguishes a 'principle of knowing (*ratio cognoscendi*, rational ground);' and under *cause* he introduces the notion of *impelling cause*, or *reason determining the will*.[14]

§11 Philosophers between Wolff and Kant

Baumgarten, in his *Metaphysics*, §§20-24, §§306-313, repeats Wolff's distinctions.

Lambert, in his *New Organon*, makes no mention of Wolff's distinctions, but in an example there shows that he distinguishes rational ground from cause when he states that God is the principle of being (*principium essendi*) of truths, while truths are God's principles of knowing (*principia cognoscendi*). (Vol. 1, §572.)

Plattner, in his *Aphorisms*, §868, says the following. 'What within the domain of representation is called ground and consequent (*principium cognoscendi, ratio — rationatum*) within the domain of reality is cause and effect (*causa efficiens — effectus*). Every cause is a rational ground, every effect a rational consequent.' What he means is that cause and effect are those elements in reality that correspond to the concepts of ground and consequent in thought. In other words, he believes that cause and effect stand to ground and consequent rather as substance and accident stand to subject and predicate, or as the quality of an object stands to the sensation that we have of it; and so on. There is no need to engage in refuting this opinion, since anyone can see that the relationship between ground and consequent in a judgment is utterly different from that apprehended as cause and effect, even if in this or that individual case what is recognised as a cause may constitute the ground of a judgment stating what the effect is (cf. §37).

Reimarus, in his *Theory of Reason*, §81, distinguishes between:

a. *inner ground*, his explanation of which accords with Wolff's explanation of reason of being (*ratio essendi*), although it would apply to rational ground (*ratio cognoscendi*) if he did not transfer to things what properly applies to concepts;

b. *outer ground* — that is, cause; at §§120ff. he correctly characterises a rational ground (*ratio cognoscendi*) as the condition of a statement, but in an example at §125 he goes on to confuse it with the notion of a cause.

§12 Kant and his school

Kant, with whom a period of world significance in the history of philosophy began, exerted a beneficial influence on logic as well as on other areas of philosophy, bringing about a more exact separation of logic from transcendental philosophy and metaphysics as practised up to his time. None the less, he introduced the principle of sufficient reason under both. In the *Logic* that bears his name he calls it the criterion of external logical truth or rationality of cognition (p. 73), on which he considers the actuality of cognition to rest (p. 75); in his transcendental logic, by contrast, he sets it forth as the principle of causality, even offering a proof of it as such; something that I shall discuss in detail in its proper place. Thus, although recognising the distinction, Kant does not give precise definitions of his expressions in keeping with it, as I shall bring out at the end of this dissertation, and so he gives rise to obscurities and misconceptions.

The various excellent textbooks of logic that have emerged from the Kantian school, those of Hofbauer, Maass, Jakob, Kiesewetter and others, all draw the distinction between rational ground and cause fairly accurately. Kiesewetter in particular, in his *Logic*, Vol. I, p. 16, states it most satisfactorily as follows: 'A ground that is logical (Erkenntnißgrund) is not to be confused with one that is real (Ursach). The principle of sufficient reason belongs to logic, that of causality to metaphysics, the former being a fundamental principle of thought, the latter of experience (p. 60). Causal ground is concerned with real things, logical ground with no more than representations.'

Kant's opponents insist even more on the distinction. G. E. Schulze, in his *Logic*, pp. 32, 84, complains of the confusion between the principle of sufficient reason and that of causality. Salomon Maimon, in his *Logic*, pp. 20f., complains that much has been said about sufficient reason without explanation of what is understood by it, and in his preface he criticises Kant for deriving the principle of causality from the logical form of hypothetical judgments (p. XXIV).

§13 On proofs of the principle

What remains to be mentioned is that various unsuccessful attempts have been made to prove the principle of sufficient reason in general, usually without a precise definition of the sense in which it is being taken; for example, Wolff, in his *Ontology*, §70, attempts a proof, which Baumgarten repeats in his *Metaphysics* (p. 7 (1783)). It would be superfluous to repeat and refute this proof here, since it so clearly rests on a play of words. Plattner in his *Aphorisms* (Vol. I, p. 322 (1793)) and Jakob in his *Logic and Metaphysics* (p. 38 (1794)) attempt other proofs, but the circularity of these is easy to discern. As to Kant's proof, there is to be a discussion of it later, as has already been said.

If I succeed in establishing in the course of this dissertation, as I hope to, what the different laws of our faculty of knowledge are, the common expression of which is the principle of sufficient reason, it will follow as a matter of course that the principle in its general form is not open to proof, and that what Aristotle said holds good of all the proofs mentioned above, with the exception of Kant's, which is meant quite differently. 'They seek a reason for things that do not have a reason; for the starting point of a demonstration is not itself a matter of demonstration.'[15] Every proof consists in showing that something we are not sure of rests upon something already established, and if we demand a proof of the latter, whatever it may be, and then go on to make similar demands at each ensuing step, we arrive in the end at principles that are the conditions of all thought and knowledge. Indeed, thought and knowledge consist in their application. Consequently, certainty is nothing more than conformity with these principles; their own certainty cannot be demonstrated by appeal to principles beyond them.

Notes

1 Ἀναγκαῖον πάντα τὰ γιγνόμενα διά τινα αἰτίαν γίγνεσθαι· πῶς γὰρ ἂν χωρὶς τούτων γίγοιτο; (*Philebus* 26e2-5.) Schopenhauer does not quote exactly here; also, a better reading is τούτου for τούτων (FW).

2 Ἐπίστασθαι δὲ οἰόμεθα ἕκαστον ἁπλῶς, ὅταν τὴν τ᾽αἰτίαν οἰόμεθα γινώσκειν δι᾽ ἣν τὸ πρᾶγμα ἔστιν, ὅτι ἐκείνου αἰτία ἐστίν, καὶ μὴ ἐνδέχεσθαι τοῦτο ἄλλως εἶναι.

3 Πασῶν μὲν οὖν κοινὸν τῶν ἀρχῶν, τὸ πρῶτον εἶναι, ὅθεν ἢ ἐστιν, ἢ γίνεται, ἢ γιγνώσκεται.

4 Αἰτίαι δὲ τέσσαρες· μία μὲν τό τι ἦν εἶναι· μία δὲ τὸ τινῶν ὄντων, ἀνάγκη τοῦτο εἶναι· ἑτέρα δέ, ἣ τι πρῶτον ἐκίνησε· τετάρτη δὲ, τὸ τίνος ἕνεκα.

5 Nulla res existit, de qua non possit quaeri, quaenam sit causa, cur existit. Hoc enim de ipso Deo quaeri potest, non quod indigeat ulla causa ut existat, sed quia ipsa ejus naturae immensitas est causa sive ratio propter quam nulla causa indiget ad existendum.

6 Ex data quacunque idea aliquis effectus necessario sequi debet.

7 Nulla res nisi a causa externa potest destrui. *Demonstratio.* Definitio cujuscunque rei, ipsius essentiam (Wesen, Beschaffenheit zum Unterschied von existentia, Dasein) affirmat, sed non negat: sive rei essentiam ponit, sed non tollit. Dum itaque ad rem ipsam tantum, non autem ad causas externas attendimus, nihil in eadem poterimus invenire, quod ipsam possit destruere.

8 Ex necessitate divinae naturae omnia quae sub intellectum infinitum cadere possunt sequi debent. (Schopenhauer's quotation is an abbreviation (FW).)

9   Quidquid existit Dei potentiam, quae omnium rerum causa est, exprimit. (This again is an abbreviation of Spinoza's sentence (FW).)

10   Deus non tantum est causa efficiens rerum existentiae, sed etiam essentiae.

11   Principium dicitur id quod in se continet rationem alterius.

12   Si lapis calescit, ignis aut radii solares sunt rationes cur calor lapidi insit.

13   In eodem exemplo, ratio possibilitatis cur lapis calorem recipere possit est in essentia seu modo compositionis lapidis.

14   Causa impulsiva, sive ratio voluntatem determinans.

15   Λόγον ζητοῦσι ὧν οὐκ ἔστι λόγος· ἀποδείξεως γὰρ οὐκ ἀποδειξίς ἐστι. (*Metaph.* 1011a, 12-13; Schopenhauer gives as reference *Metaph.* III, 6 (FW).)

3 Insufficiency of the account given so far and an outline of a new one

§14 Cases not included in the meanings of the principle already presented

The general outcome of the summary presented in the last chapter is that philosophers have distinguished two applications of the principle of sufficient reason, although they have done so only step by step and not without frequently falling back into confusion and error. The first application concerns judgments: a judgment must always have a reason if it is to be true. The second concerns changes in real objects: every such change must have a cause. In both cases we find that the principle justifies our asking why, a characteristic essential to it.

Are all cases in which we are justified in asking *why* contained under these two relations? Let us suppose that I ask, 'Why are the three sides of this triangle equal?' The answer is, 'Because its three angles are equal.' Is the equality of the angles then the *cause* of the equality of the sides? No. For there is no question of a change here, no question of an effect requiring a cause. Is it then a mere rational ground that is at stake? No. For the equality of the angles does not merely establish the equality of the sides; it does not constitute the mere rational ground of a judgment. In short, there is no way of grasping simply from the concepts that the sides must be equal if the angles are; the concept of the equality of a triangle's sides is not encompassed within that of the equality of its angles. What is at issue is not a relation between concepts and judgments, but between sides and angles. The equality of the angles is not *directly* the ground of our *knowing* the equality of the sides but only *indirectly*: it is the ground of something's *being such and such*, in this case the ground of the sides' being equal. The sides must be equal because the angles are. We have here then a necessary relation between angles and sides, not directly a relation between judgments. To take another example: if I ask,

'Why are you doing that?' you will give me a motive. Will this motive be a cause and the ensuing action its effect? No. For no motive can be cited from which the action follows with necessity, whereas the relation between cause and effect is one of necessity. Will the motive then be a rational ground, with the action as its consequent? No. For what is in question is not an act of cognition but a preceding change.

§15 All applications of the principle must be capable of division into definite sorts

We see from the above examples that not all applications of the principle of sufficient reason are reducible to rational ground and consequent or cause and effect. Consequently, a division assuming that they are would not comply with the law of specification. On the other hand, if we accept the law of homogeneity, we must take for granted that applications of the principle are not infinite in variety but capable of division into sorts.

Before attempting any such division, though, I need to determine what are the characteristics common to the principle in all cases. That is, I need to establish the concept of the genus before that of the species.

§16 The root of the principle of sufficient reason

Our consciousness, to the extent that it manifests itself as sensibility, understanding and reason, is divided into subject and object; considered thus far it comprises nothing further. To be object for a subject and to be representation is one and the same thing. All representations are objects for a subject, all objects for a subject are representations. But nothing can become an object for us that exists of itself and independently, nothing that exists in isolation and apart. On the contrary, all representations stand in a relation of interconnectedness that in respect of form is governed by a rule determinable a priori. It is this interconnectedness that constitutes the relation expressed by the principle of sufficient reason understood generally; and it is this rule governing all representations that is the root of the principle of sufficient reason and constitutes the matter of fact underlying it. The principle expresses this matter of fact, but generally we have access to it in the form in which it is presented here only as a result of abstraction. In the concrete it is presented to us through individual cases.

NOTE. All statements made here will be argued for and elucidated in the following sections of the dissertation, and a clear understanding of the root of the principle of sufficient reason will be attained through an examination of its four parts.

§17 Its fourfold nature

The previously mentioned cases revealing the law of necessary interconnectedness among representations are cases in which the principle of sufficient reason expressing that law finds application. On closer examination, carried out in accordance with the laws of homogeneity and specification, the principle is found to divide into specific and very distinct species. There are *four* such species, I believe, and they are dependent upon the *four classes* into which all things fall that are capable of becoming objects for us; in other words, they are dependent upon our representations. These classes will be enumerated and discussed in the following four chapters.

Since the appearance of Kant's deduction of the categories, virtually nothing is considered to be so basic and immediate that it may not be furnished with an a priori deduction. Indeed, things that previous generations never hoped to trace back to ultimate grounds have now been treated in a manner recalling the words of Goethe:

The philosopher steps in,
And proves to you that it must be so.

In the light of this, it may well be expected that I shall not fail to provide an a priori deduction justifying my division. But I confess to discerning no possibility of such a deduction for the four classes of representations that alone are given to us: any attempt at one would lack basis or content, even if it managed to scare off the sceptic through its sheer boringness. I fear that in trying for such a justification I should too much recall the inflated wineskins at Apuleius' door, suspended there to make him think, when returning home drunk and seeing them swinging in the wind, that they were robbers about to break in.[1]

So I base my division of representations upon induction, and the only thing that I can do by way of proof is to challenge anyone to come forward with an object not belonging to one of the classes enumerated, or to demonstrate that any two of them are really *but one.*

I draw attention in passing to the fact that even Kant's list of categories is based upon induction. It was drawn up from the logical table of judgments, and the division of the characteristics of these into four species each comprising three sorts is based solely upon induction. Kant himself indicates this when in drawing up the table he says: 'If we consider the pure form of the understanding in the judgments, *we find* that the functions of thought can be brought under four heads.' (*CPR,* p. 95.) And in the same work he says: 'Our understanding possesses the characteristic of being able to bring about unity of apperception a priori only by means of the categories, and moreover only by means of these particular kinds and this particular number of categories. But we can no more account for this characteristic than we can for having these and no other functions of judgment, or for possessing only space and time as forms of possible intuition.' (*CPR,* p. 145.) As to Kant's *deduction,* this is not in any sort a demonstration that the categories must be such as they are and as many as they are; rather, it is 'the explanation of how a priori concepts can apply to objects.' Consequently, not only is a deduction unnecessary for the present division of possible objects for a subject, but a request for one lacks sense and meaning. The division, as has been noted already, is based solely upon induction.

The principle of sufficient reason assumes a different form in each of the four classes of objects for our faculty of representation shortly to be named. But, allowing as it does of the single expression referred to earlier on, it is revealed as one and the same principle and as issuing from the root (referred to in Section 16) whose fourfold nature becomes clear from a consideration of the principle's four forms.

14

While naming each of the classes of representations, I shall state which form of the principle of sufficient reason holds within it as its law of connectedness.

Note

1   *Metamorph.*, II in fine and III initio.

4 On the first class of objects for the subject and the form of the principle of sufficient reason governing it

§18 General account of this class of objects

The first class of possible objects for our faculty of representation is the class of *complete representations constituting the totality of an experience*. The principle of sufficient reason holding within it assumes the form of the law of causality, of which more will be said later.

To say that representations belonging to this class are *complete* means, to make use of the distinction made by Kant, that they comprise both *material* and *formal* elements of sensible appearances. That they constitute a *totality of experience* means that they stand in a relation of connectedness knowable only through the understanding. Consequently, they are the work of our entire sensibility and understanding, and constitute what is called the *objective, real world*.

§19 Outline of an analysis of experience: the understanding

The forms of representations of this first class are the forms of inner and outer sense, *time* and *space*, though we can be *aware* of these only if they are possessed of content. A detailed consideration of their *apprehensibility*, namely *matter*, will have to wait till later on (§42); here it will be taken for granted.

If time were the unique form of representations of this class, we should have no knowledge of *coexistence*, nor consequently of *permanence* or *duration*. For *time* is apprehended only in so far as it possesses content, and its

16

course is apprehended only through *changes* in that content. An object's *permanence*, therefore, is recognised only by contrast with *changes* taking place in objects *coexisting* with it. However, the representation of *coexistence* is impossible in time alone: the representation of *space* is needed to complete it. For while everything in time taken in isolation is *successive*, in space things rest *side by side*. But this does not mean to say that things *coexist* in space; in space as such there is no coexistence, any more than there is a before and after. And while before and after are possible only through time, *coexistence* is possible only through the representations of time and space united.

If space were the only form of representations of this class, we should have no knowledge of *change*, since change or alteration is constituted by *successions* of states, and these are only possible in time.

Consequently, although both forms of complete representations, as we know, are alike in possessing infinite divisibility and extension, they are fundamentally different in that what is essential to *one* has no meaning when ascribed to the *other*. 'Next to' is without meaning in time, 'succession' without meaning in space. Complete representations, however, constituting the totality of an experience, appear under both forms simultaneously: a *close union* between the two is indeed a prerequisite of experience, which grows out of them rather as products in arithmetic grow out of their factors.

What brings this *union* about is the *understanding*, its *categories* being the various means of its performing its function; it creates *experience* by bringing about a close union between the above mentioned heterogeneous forms of sensibility, thereby producing a *total representation*.

Within this total representation everything else belonging to this class is contained, governed by determinate laws known to us a priori; within it innumerable representations commonly referred to as objects now *coexist*; within it substance acquires permanence, despite the fact that time cannot be halted, while the states of substance succeed one another, despite the rigid immovability of space. Within it, in a word, the whole objective, real world exists for us.

It would be a singularly laborious and difficult task, and one well beyond my present purposes, to undertake a thorough examination of all this, providing a detailed explanation of the manner in which the understanding brings about the above mentioned union and experience: providing, in other words, a complete analysis of experience. Kant says something about it in his transcendental analytic of the pure understanding, and although what he says constitutes no more than a preliminary study, it is none the less important. By attentively considering his individual categories and the relations they bear to the forms of sensibility, anyone may convince himself of the truth of Kant's general position. Further, anyone may be persuaded by his novel account of the understanding, which in the following chapter he distinguishes from reason — likewise given a novel account — more precisely than others before him.

§20 Immediate presence of representations

Although the understanding unites the forms of inner and outer sense to produce a complete representation of an experience, the subject has *imme-*

diate knowledge only through the *inner sense* — while the outer sense constitutes an object for the inner sense, and the inner sense in turn apprehends what is apprehended by the outer. Consequently, in respect of the *immediate presence* of representations to consciousness, the subject comes under the conditions of *time* alone, the form of *inner sense*. For this reason, a subject can be presented with only *one* clear representation at a time, even if that representation comprises many elements. Moreover, for two reasons that representation always disappears, superseded by another in accordance with a rule that is not determinable a priori but dependent upon circumstances shortly to be looked into. The first of these reasons is that the subject will not stay with that *unique* representation: given the laws governing the world of experience, it cannot do so. The other reason is that in time by itself there is no coexistence.

In spite of this transitory nature and separateness of representations in respect of their immediate presence before the subject's consciousness, there exists for the subject the representation of a totality of experience, brought about by the operation of the understanding in the manner explained above. But, because of the contrast between representations seen on the one hand as belonging to the complete representation of experience and representations seen on the other hand as immediately present to consciousness, the two have been taken to be quite different. The first have been spoken of as *real things*, the second as representations pure and simple. However, to speak in this way is to overlook the fact that the so-called existence of real things is *nothing other than their being represented*. (At any rate, the existence of real things is identical with their being represented *potentially*,[1] for those who insist that only the immediate presence in the consciousness of a subject is to be called being represented *actually*.[2]) In short, it is to overlook that an object is *nothing* without its relation to a subject: nothing remains when that relation is removed or considered in abstraction, and the attribution of *absolute existence* to an object is an absurdity from the start, deserving of no serious consideration.

Leibniz was unable to free himself from the idea that an object has absolute existence, independently of its relation to a subject — in other words, independently of its *being represented* — and when he wished to define that existence more accurately, he found himself driven to asserting that objects are subjects, *monades*. In so doing he furnished the most eloquent proof that within the confines of sense, understanding and reason, our consciousness knows nothing but subject and object, representer and represented. For if we abstract from the objective existence of an object, from its being represented, and consequently annul it as an object, yet at the same time wish to preserve something, we come up with mere *subject*. By contrast, if we wish to abstract from the subjective existence of a subject, while again not wishing to be left with nothing, we again come up with the opposite. This time we come up with *materialism*.

It was quite clear to Spinoza that the necessary relation between subject and object is fundamental, an absolute condition of their conceivability; and for this reason he defined the relation between the thought and extension that characterises the sole existing substance as a relation of identity.

More detailed considerations will be given to this identity between subjective and objective later on (§42). For the moment it is enough to note

18

the following. The distinction between subject and object, between that which knows but is never known and that which is known but never knows, is the most fundamental distinction that we are able to come to grips with. An indication of it even appears in a number of languages, the words for 'am' and 'is' having different roots.[3] However, the infinitive, *to be*, unites the two meanings under the single concept of *being*, by virtue of which, the knowing subject, I, and the table at which I am now writing both share a common predicate. But this concept of *being* is the progenitor of many and self-multiplying errors, and it consequently allows for the establishing of a whole genealogy of error. For example, on the assumption that the two meanings of the progenitor apply to them, from the concept of *being* stem the concepts of *substance, realities, perfections,* and many others, from which in turn emerge offspring of the most varied kinds: for example, from *substance* emerge such offspring as *dualism, Spinozism, rational psychology.*

This fact that the concept of *being*, expressed in the infinitive *to be*, goes inevitably with language and indeed almost with our use of reason, is one of the many proofs of the fact that so little in us is directed towards knowing. In fact everything is directed towards willing, so that, while as knowers we remain children, as willers we may be giants at any age.

NOTE. With reference to the main argument of this section, I draw attention to the fact that in the course of my dissertation I make use of the expression *real objects*, for the sake of brevity and clarity. But I wish to state here once and for all that nothing is to be understood by that expression except complete representations, integrated within a totality of experience.

§21 Of the immediate object

We have seen that by virtue of the nature of inner sense, the sense that belongs to the subject as the condition of apprehension, only a series of representations that is both simple in the sense of not allowing of coexistence and fleeting in the sense of not possessing anything permanent can be *immediately present* to the subject. And by saying that representations are *immediately* present is meant that they are not simply known in the unity of time and space which constitutes the totality of experience brought about by the understanding, but, as representations of the inner sense, in time alone.

The condition referred to above for the immediate presence of a representation that belongs to the first class of objects is that it should stand in a causal relation to a representation of the kind that I refer to as *immediate*. This immediate representation is determinate and complete, and it belongs to the totality of experience. I refer to it as *immediate* to contrast it with other complete representations to which it stands as *medium*.

This representation is *one's own body*. It is the *immediate object*, and as one object among others it comes under the law of causality governing the first class of representations. Only as a result of changes brought about in a subject by other objects are these immediately present to it, and what we call their existence is nothing other than their ability to be thus immediately present to a subject. It is important to note, however, that it is not simply an effect brought about by other objects that is apprehended, not simply a modification produced by them in the immediate object.

19

Were this the case, there would be only *one* object for a subject — namely, the immediate object itself with its changing states. On the contrary, through the operations of the understanding as applied to the forms of sensibility, which in this class of representations are not encountered without the material element, there is also apprehended the cause of the effect produced. It is apprehended as the substratum underlying a power, as a substance and as present in space. What this means is that *the other objects are apprehended as belonging to the totality of experience just as is the immediate object itself.*

That this or that object can become causally related to the immediate object depends upon a number of circumstances: the location of the two in space, the medium in which they are to be found, the receptiveness of the immediate object (the soundness of its senses), and so forth.

NOTE 1. The concept of causality has had to be anticipated here, although an account of it will not be given until the second half of the chapter.

NOTE 2. It is worth noting, for the sake of having a thorough understanding of what is said in this section, that all parts of the immediate object become mediate objects in turn, given that parts of it can affect others. For example, my hand is an immediate object for me when through its touch I recognise the effect of another object upon it, and as a result of this recognise it as something present in space. By contrast, my hand is a mediate object when I see it: when, as a result of light rays reflected from it on to my eye, I recognise its effectiveness, its reality, its occupancy of space. My eye, which just now was an immediate object, becomes mediate when I touch it or do something else of the sort. It is easy to see, further, that if among objects presented to me mediately I discover some of a quality similar to that of my *immediate* object, I conclude that these too are immediate objects for a subject; even if the similarity in question is not too close, as in the case of animals. Plants provide grounds for supposing that, while they are certainly immediate, they are not mediating objects for a subject: that is, that they have life, but not sensibility.

§22 Mental images and dreams: the imagination

Once a subject has had representations immediately present to it through its immediate object, it is able to recall these without mediation, merely by choosing to do so. It can even change their order and the way in which they stand to one another. Repetitions of such a kind I call *mental images*, and their faculty the *phantasy* or *imagination*. Given what was said in Section 18, these representations are certainly *complete*; on the other hand, not *belonging to the totality of experience*, they do not fall under the law of causality governing that totality. Rather, given that they are products of choice, they fall under the law of motivation governing the final class of objects for the faculty of representation.

I mention these representations here because in virtue of being complete this is where they belong: by contrast, in virtue of being matters of choice they fall under a different law from that governing the totality of experience. I also mention them here because as *mental images* they are to be distinguished from *concepts*, which will be dealt with in the next chapter.

Our ability to distinguish mental images from real objects is to be explained in the following way. When we are awake, our *immediate object* is *immediately present* to our consciousness without interruption. By contrast, other representations belonging to the totality of experience are immediately present to us only while a change is occurring in the immediate object which causes them to be present to us; moreover, and as a consequence, this change itself is included as *an integral part* in the representation belonging to the totality of experience present to us at any given moment. In similar fashion, mental images include representations of changes — as repetitions — occurring in the immediate object, together with the operations of the understanding that are applied to changes of this sort, just as they are applied to real changes.

However, the livelier a mental image is in such a case, the weaker for the moment is the direct presence to consciousness of the immediate object. None the less, the immediate object normally remains present in such a way that while mental images including changes in the immediate object become objects for us, at the same time we are aware of the immediate object as if it were *without* such changes. On the other hand, when mental images reach such a pitch of liveliness that they force the immediate object from consciousness altogether, it is only through re-entry of the immediate object into consciousness that we recognise mental images for what they are; a re-entry that is bound to occur, because the immediate object, being a representation belonging to the totality of experience and falling under its laws, is something that *perdures*.

This is the only way that we have of recognising mental images of a very vivid sort, since it is normally impossible for us to view the immediate object as one among many in the complex of experience and subject to the rule (yet to be discussed) that every event must occupy a place in a series of causes and effects. It is normally impossible for us to realise, therefore, as a result of applying the laws governing experience, that the immediate object could not have undergone this or that effect whose representation is included in a mental image. This is because we can rarely pursue a series of causes and effects very far, and certainly never through to the end. Let me illustrate the point. If I imagine that someone has entered my room, I can recognise this as a case of imagination only in the first way mentioned, through the re-entry into consciousness of my immediate object. For, inquiries into the circumstances preceding such a supposed entry rarely get far.

When we are asleep, our immediate object is withdrawn from consciousness, together with everything mediated through it; and, given that there is no subject where there is no object, this explains the occurrence of sleep without consciousness. Mental images, on the other hand, unmediated repetitions of representations that otherwise demand mediation, are possible even in sleep. They are known as *dreams*.

As our immediate object is removed from consciousness in sleep, we are not able to distinguish mental images from real objects, because the criterion mentioned earlier is wanting. Consequently, it is only at the point of waking, when the immediate object re-enters consciousness, that we are able to recognise mental images as such — a re-entry that *has* to occur, owing to the fact that representations belonging to the totality of experience continue in existence independently of their immediate presence in consciousness. It follows that waking is the sole criterion for distinguishing dreams from reality.

There are occasions when we forget the moment of waking, and doubt whether this or that event has taken place or was merely dreamed. On such occasions we are obliged to have recourse to the much less reliable inquiry into whether the event in question occupied a place in a chain of causes and effects.

§23 The principle of sufficient reason of becoming

The class of objects for the subject that were described at the beginning of this chapter is governed by the principle of sufficient reason in the form of *the law of causality*, and as such I refer to it as *the principle of sufficient reason of becoming*, principium rationis sufficientis fiendi. Through it, all representations contained within the complete representation that we call experience are linked together. If a new state of a real object or of several real objects comes into being, this state must follow another that preceded it according to a rule: whenever the first comes into being, the second follows. A sequence of this kind is called a *result*, the first state being termed a *cause*, the second an *effect*. To take an example, if a body catches fire, the state of burning is necessarily preceded by a state comprising the following: i) exposition to oxygen; ii) contact with oxygen; iii) specific temperature. Once the latter complex state is present, necessarily combustion takes place. Moreover, it occurs at a particular moment, so that the complex state itself cannot have been permanently in existence, but must follow from one preceding it. For example, it must follow from the application of free heat to the body, from which a rise in temperature necessarily ensues. This application of heat is in turn determined by a preceding state, such as the incidence of sunrays upon a burning-glass; this perhaps by the removal of a cloud from before the sun; this by the wind; this by a difference of density in the air; this by further states; and so on indefinitely.

When all conditions *but one* for the existence of a new state are present, and this one finally arrives at the end of the line, it is likely to be referred to as the cause *par excellence* — a way of speaking that is acceptable enough in ordinary conversation but is none the less inaccurate. For the fact that a particular condition for the existence of a given state is the last to occur invests it with no special standing, and there is consequently no justification for calling the removal of a cloud the cause of combustion simply because it occurs later than the focusing of the burning-glass. This is because that focusing could have occurred later than the removal of the cloud, and the addition of oxygen could have occurred even later still. If the customary way of speaking were adhered to, then, temporal conditions that are accidental would decide what the cause is. What we find on closer consideration is that the *entire complex state* constitutes the condition of what follows, the temporal order of its components being unimportant.

A further point to note is that this customary way of speaking is accompanied by another, one that is badly mistaken in referring to objects rather than states as causes. To illustrate the point by reference to the example given above: some would call the burning-glass the cause of the combustion, others the cloud, others the sun, others the oxygen — preferences that are arbitrary and without rule. Further, there is really no sense to saying that one object is the cause of another. Causality is a relation between two *states*, one being termed the *cause*, the other the *effect*, while the sequence is termed the *result*. And, to mention the point in passing, given that the law of causality applies to states, not things, and that only states appear and disappear, pass into being and out of being, the principle of the permanence of substance follows immediately from an analysis of the concept of causality. No synthesis is required.

Given that any state must follow another according to a rule and unfailingly, the relation between cause and effect is one of necessity, and in virtue of this the law of causality constitutes a basis for hypothetical judgments, thereby showing itself to be a form of the principle of sufficient reason, upon which all hypothetical judgments must rest.

I call this particular form of the principle the principle of sufficient reason of *becoming*, because its application everywhere presupposes a change, a becoming. A further presupposition of the principle is that a cause must precede its effect in time (cf. §53), an aspect of it that enables us to tell which of two causally related states is cause, which effect.

§24 Arguments against Kant's proof of this principle, and the setting forth of a new proof written in the same spirit

One of the chief aims of the *Critique of Pure Reason* is to explain the universal application of the law of causality to experience, to explain its restriction to experience, and to explain its a priori nature. It is unnecessary to repeat what is said there, and, given that in general I myself appeal to what Kant says, I wish to discuss but one point that I cannot agree with, namely the proof of the a priori nature of the principle of causality.

First a preliminary remark. Kant takes the principle of sufficient reason to be identical with the law of causality (*CPR*, p. 246), while Salomon Maimon takes the opposite view (*Logic*, p. 24), as do Kiesewetter (*Logic*, p. 16) and G. E. Schulze (*Logic*, pp. 32, 84). I myself am with Kant on this. On the other hand, as I argue throughout this dissertation, I hold that the law of causality is one of four modifications or forms of the principle of sufficient reason.

On the page referred to above, Kant presents a proof of the principle of sufficient reason that in substance goes as follows. 'The imagination's synthesis of the manifold needed for empirical knowledge gives rise to succession, but not immediately to determinate succession: it leaves indeterminate which of two apprehended states comes first, not only in the imagination but in the object itself. Determinate order, through which alone what is apprehended becomes experience — that is, through which alone are provided grounds for objectively valid judgments — only makes its entry through the concepts of cause and effect, which belong to the pure understanding. Thus the basic principle of causal relation is the condition of the possibility of experience, and as such it is given to us a priori.'

It should first be noted that this proof concerns the law of causality, not the principle of sufficient reason in general; the latter, as I hope to demonstrate, has three further and quite distinct applications or forms. I agree with Kant that the law of causality in conjunction with the other categories — that is, with the understanding in general — makes possible the totality of objective knowledge referred to as experience. (Section 42 provides further explanation of this.) However, I believe that the understanding procures this by uniting time and space through the categories, not by means of the categories alone. In other words, it is not experience that is given to the understanding by itself, but only the laws that are known to it a priori. Experience itself is the union of time and space brought about through the understanding, and it can therefore only be apprehended through the *joint* employment of the understanding and sensibility. Consequently, I cannot accept that the order in which sequences of changes occur in real objects is recognised as objective solely by means of the category of causality. Kant asserts several times in the *Critique of Pure Reason* that this is so, and gives explanations of this assertion (esp. pp. 232-256, 264).

I ask anyone wishing to understand what I have to say to look up the relevant passages of the *Critique*. Kant asserts there that the *objectivity of sequences of representations*, which he explains as their correspondence with sequences of real objects, is known solely through the law that they obey in following one another, namely the law of causality. He affirms that in pure apprehension the objective relation of phenomena following one another remains indeterminate, since what are apprehended in this way are merely sequences of our own representations. But sequences thus apprehended, he asserts, furnish us with no grounds for making judgments about corresponding sequences in objects, unless those judgments appeal to the law of causality; for we can reverse the order of the contents of what we apprehend, given that there is nothing to determine them as objective.

To illustrate his point, Kant takes the example of a house, whose parts he can consider in any order that he cares: from top to bottom, say, or from bottom to top. Such a determining of order is purely subjective, he holds, since it depends upon his choice, not upon what is objective. As an example of the opposite, he cites watching a ship sailing down a river, first seeing it high upstream and then progressively lower down, while remaining at all points unable to alter its successive locations. In this second case, Kant considers the subjective sequence of apprehensions to be based upon an objective sequence existing in phenomena, and consequently he calls it an *event*.

I assert, on the contrary, that *there is no difference between the cases. Both are events*, and knowledge of both is objective; that is, knowledge of both is knowledge of changes in real objects and recognised to be such by the subject.

Both are cases of change in relative position between objects. In the first case, one of the objects is the immediate object: to be more precise, it is a part of the immediate object, the eye. The other object is one that is known indirectly, through the immediate object, and consists of those parts of the house in relation to which the position of the eye progressively changes. In the second case, where the ship's position relative to the river changes, the change is between two objects that are known indirectly, through the immediate object.

So in both cases the sequences are events, the only difference being that in the first case the change is between an immediate object and one that is mediate, while in the second it is between objects both of which are mediate. If the observer were able to pull the ship upstream as he is

24

able to reverse the movements of his eye, the order in which the changes occur could as easily be reversed in the second as in the first case.

From the fact that the sequence in which the parts of the house are perceived is a matter of choice, Kant concludes that it is not objective and therefore not an event. But this is wrong. The movement of the eye from roof to basement or from basement to roof is just as much an event as the sailing of the ship, and there is no greater difference between them than between my passing a line of soldiers and their passing me. Both are events.

Kant would not have imagined there to be a difference had he reflected on the following. The body is an object among objects, and a sequence of immediately present, complete representations that are not mental images depends upon a sequence of impressions made by other objects upon the immediate object. It is this that makes the sequence of representations objective, one taking place among objects and not, or at least not *directly*, the outcome of choice. Such a sequence, therefore, is not difficult to recognise, independently of whether or not the objects successively acting upon the immediate object are causally interrelated.

Kant asserts that we cannot be empirically aware of time, and that consequently there are no sequences of representations that we can apprehend empirically as objective: in other words, no sequences of changes among phenomena that we can distinguish from changes among purely subjective representations. It is only through the law of causality, in accordance with which states follow one another regularly, that we discern the objectivity of a change. If Kant were right, we should apprehend no sequences in time as objective other than sequences of cause and effect; all other sequences of phenomena would be determined solely by choice. But Kant is not right. Phenomena can *follow upon* one another without *resulting from* one another, and this in no way threatens the law of causality, which remains certain and presupposed a priori.

Every change is the effect of another; but this does not mean that a change follows its cause and nothing else. Rather, every change follows all other changes that occur simultaneously with its cause without being causally related to it; and because of this we apprehend changes as belonging not to causal sequences but to sequences of a different kind. But this does not render them any less objective. They are objective, and we apprehend them as distinct from subjective sequences which depend upon choice; for example, as distinct from sequences of mental images.

A sequence of events in time that are not causally related is called a *coincidence*, a word derived from the falling together or coinciding of unconnected events. To illustrate the point, let us suppose that a tile falls from the roof as I am going out of my house, and that it hits me. No causal link exists between the falling of the tile and my going out, but the sequence of my going out and the falling of the tile is none the less determined objectively in my apprehension; not subjectively, by my choosing. Indeed, had I been able to choose, I should doubtless have chosen a different sequence of events.

In exactly the same way, the sequence of notes in a piece of music is determined objectively, not subjectively by the listener; yet no one would assert that the notes therefore follow in causal sequence. Even the rotation of the earth, the sequence serving as our standard for other sequences, is undoubtedly recognised by us as objective, but not because we apply the concept of causality to it; indeed the cause of this sequence is unknown to us.

According to Kant, we can interpret representations as evidence for the existence of objective reality (by contrast with mental images and mere concepts, I take him to mean) only when we recognise them as necessarily connected with other representations, and subject like them to a rule, namely the law of causality, as well as being located in a determinate order in the temporal chain of our representations (pp. 242f.). To this I must object. There are not many representations whose place in the lawlike sequence of cause and effect is known to us; but we always know how to distinguish objective from subjective representations, real objects from mental images. For, as I showed in Section 22, we are fully aware when, on the one hand, representations are mediated through the immediate object and when, on the other hand, they are produced without mediation and freely chosen as repetitions. In our dreams, by contrast, when the immediate object is removed from consciousness, we cannot make this distinction, and take mental images to be real objects, only discovering our error when we wake up, when the immediate object re-enters our consciousness. Yet our dreams surely come under the law of causality.

Kant's proof of the a priori nature and necessity of the law of causality derives from his claim that it is only through the law of causality that we can recognise the objective sequence of changes, thus making causality the condition of all experience. I cannot accept this, though I do agree that we have a priori awareness of the rule according to which changes in states of real objects necessarily follow one another, and I also agree with the conclusions that Kant draws from this.

It seems to me that the proof of our a priori awareness of the law of causality is to be found in the unshakeable certainty with which we expect experience in all cases to conform to it; that is, in the apodeictic certainty that we ascribe to it. This certainty is not the same as that based upon induction (e.g., the certainty that we have of empirically known laws of nature), since it is impossible to make sense of the idea that the law of causality might have exceptions in the world of experience. To illustrate the point, we can *make sense of the idea* that in some circumstances the law of gravitation might fail to apply, but not of the idea that such a failure might occur without a cause.

However, there is also a *proof* of the kind desired by Kant, a way of showing that experience is impossible without the law of causality. It goes as follows. Only *one* object is given to us *immediately*, namely our body, and it is impossible to understand how we get beyond this to other objects in space if not through the category of causality. For without this we would be confronted merely with the immediate object and its succeeding states. In other words, without the application of the understanding there would be nothing but sensation. There would be no perception, since perception — at any rate, perception of objects as opposed to pure perception of time and space — is nothing other than the union of time and space, given content and brought about through the categories. Nothing is given to us immediately other than the immediate object located in space, together with the sequences of its states in time. Indeed, the immediate object itself is an *object* only through an application of the categories of subsistence, reality, unity, and so on.

26

By contrast, knowledge of *mediate* objects comes into being through the category of causality. A cause is inferred from changes occurring in the eye, ear or some other organ of sense, and is located in space in the region where its activity originates, as a substratum of its power to produce such activity. It is only then that the categories of subsistence, existence, and so on, can be applied. Consequently, the category of causality is the true point of transition, and therefore the *condition of all experience*. As such it does not have its origin in experience, but precedes it; for it is only through the category of causality that we recognise objects as *real* (wirklich), that is as *having effects* upon us (auf uns wirkend), and the fact that we are unconscious of the inference we make here should not be seen as a difficulty, any more than the unconscious inference that we make from a body's shading to its shape. The inference in question here is not one of reason, resulting from the conjoining of judgments, since it is not the concept of the category that we are dealing with, but the category it-self, which leads directly from effect to cause.[4] Because of this, our consciousness of the operations of causality differs from that of the operations of the other categories only in this, that it is through the other categories that our consciousness emerges from vague sensation to perception.

I wish to call this form of inference that does not make use of abstract concepts, and consequently does not make use of minor premises, the inference of the understanding. In logic this is a name given to a kind of inference that clearly is not different enough to warrant being assigned to a distinct mental faculty, and, given the sharp distinction that I have established between the understanding and reason, the name as thus employed in logic is unsuitable.

There are many who deny the existence of this sort of inference altogether; for example, Fries in his recent *Critique of Reason*, Vol. I, pp. 52-56, 290, and Schelling in the first volume of his *Writings*, pp. 237f. But there is a tangible proof of it, tangible moreover in the most direct sense of the word. If you cross your middle-finger and your index-finger, and run the two over the surface of a ball, you will be certain that you are feeling two balls, only sight convincing you that there *is but one*. (This striking case of illusion attracted the attention of Aristotle (*Met.* III, 6).) You will be convinced that you are apprehending two balls, and apprehending them moreover by means of the most infallible sense and in the most direct manner possible, while in fact your conviction is based upon an inference which, if conceptualised, would go as follows.

- If two spherical surfaces simultaneously affect the outer sides of the middle-finger and index-finger, it cannot be a *single* ball that is having this effect.
- That is what is happening now.
- Therefore, there are two balls here now.

This argument is fallacious, since the natural position of the fingers presupposed in the major premiss is inverted.

Kant seems to have fallen into an error exactly opposite to Hume's. For whereas Hume declared all consequence to be mere sequence, Kant wants all sequence to be consequence. The pure understanding can, it is true, grasp *consequence* by itself, but it cannot in that way grasp pure *sequence*, any more than it can grasp the difference between right and left. Pure sequence, like the difference between right and left, can only be apprehended through the faculty of pure sensibility. Sequences of events in time, like contiguity of things in space, can be known empirically (though on page 233 Kant denies this), but the manner in which one thing *follows* another in time can no more be accounted for than the manner in which one thing is the *consequence* of another. Knowledge of the first is given and conditioned by pure sensibility, knowledge of the second by pure understanding. In declaring that the objective sequence of phenomena cannot be known without the introduction of causality, Kant falls into the very error that he reproaches *Leibniz* with. 'He intellectualises the forms of sensibility.' (*CPR*, p. 331.)

Concerning succession, my own opinion is this. We create knowledge of the bare *possibility* of succession out of the form of time which belongs to pure sensibility. We know of the *succession* of real objects, whose form is time, empirically and therefore as *real*. Finally, we know of the *necessity* of the succession of two states, of a change, only through the understanding and by means of the category of causality. Indeed, the very fact that we possess the concept of the necessity of succession is proof that the law of causality is known not empirically but a priori.

When taken in its general sense, the principle of sufficient reason expresses the necessity binding together all objects or representations, a necessity lying deep within the faculty of knowledge; while the principle appearing as the law of causality governing the present class of representations conditions sequences that are temporal, because time is the form of those representations. It is owing to this, then, that the necessary connection appears here as a rule of succession in time, while in other cases it appears under forms different from time, and that in these other cases the principle is not concerned with succession. But in all cases the character of necessary connection is retained, and it is through this that the identity of the principle in all its forms is revealed, or rather that the unity of the root of the laws expressed by it is revealed.

If the assertion made by Kant and disputed here were correct, we should apprehend the *reality* of succession only in apprehending its *necessity*; but that would require omniscience embracing all causal series. In other words, Kant is imposing an impossibility on the understanding merely to have less need of sensibility. In any event, how could his assertion that we know the objectivity of succession only when we know the necessity with which effect follows upon cause be reconciled with his assertion that the empirical criterion for deciding which of two states is cause and which is effect is simply succession? (*CPR*, p. 249.) The circularity involved here will escape no one.

If we could know of the objectivity of a succession only by recognising it to be causal, we should not be able to think of it as anything but causal. What is more, it would not in fact be anything but causal, since otherwise it would possess additional characteristics enabling it to be recognised, and this is precisely what Kant denies. If Kant were right, then, we should not be able to say things like, 'This state is the effect of that, and therefore follows it.' For sequence and effect would be the same, making such a statement tautological. In addition, Hume would be proved right in having denied the distinction between sequence and consequence when he declared all consequence to be sequence.

28

In the end, Kant's entire doctrine on the issue rests on the following false dilemma. If representations succeed one another, either this is the result of choice or it is in accordance with a rule. But this is not so. Representations can succeed one another with a necessity that is not rule-governed, a necessity in virtue of which countless objects affect my body in succession owing to their common form of time. Moreover, given that my body is one among many objects governed by the law of causality, it is able to receive effects from without; and these effects must be known to me as occurring successively, since my body itself is known to me in time.

Let us finally ask the following question. If the objectivity of succession or change is known solely through causality, how is the objectivity of duration known? This is important, because it is on account of duration as much as change that time is posited as a condition of representations, not only as these are immediately present to consciousness, but as they belong to the total representation of experience. We know of time, not only in the immediate presence of representations to our consciousness, but in the belonging of these to the total representation of experience, or — to use ordinary language — we know of time as a condition of real objects, because our immediate objects as much as others belong to the world of objects, and successive changes in them are given as immediately as they themselves. But these changes presuppose time, not only as the form of representations immediately present to us, but as the form of representations existing within the total representation of an experience.

Kant's proof of the a priori nature of the law of causality, then, needs qualification. Empirically we recognise no more than that succession is *real*. But we also recognise in certain series of events that succession is *necessary* — we even know ahead of experience that all possible events must have a determinate place in one or other of these series — and it is from this that it follows at once that the law of causality is both real and a priori in nature. (Incidentally, the proof that I presented above as meeting Kant's own requirements puts this beyond doubt.) I agree with Kant, then, that the apprehension of a succession of states belonging to real objects is *accompanied* by the presupposition of a cause; I merely deny that it is *conditioned* by that presupposition. I also agree with him that every event belongs to a series in which its position is determined in accordance with a rule and is therefore necessary. But I do not agree with him that we discover the place of a given event in time solely from our knowledge of the law of causality and from the position of that event in a series. In other words, I do not agree that we are unable to discover the place of a given event empirically. For there are countless series of causes and effects, the members of each of which bear a temporal relation that is objective (existing in the totality of experience) and therefore knowable, a relation not only to one another but to members of every other series, even though they are not causally related to them. Of course, the temporal relation of members to one another *within a single* series is knowable a priori through the law of causality, and it is therefore determined that members of a single series cannot coexist. But the temporal relation of members of one series to those of *another* can only be known empirically, through the form of time, which makes possible not only representations immediately present to the subject, but complete representations that have to coexist with many others within the totality of experience.

All of this may be symbolised by the figure of a plane circle representing time when time is *possessed of content*. The centre of the circle stands for the present, its countless radii stand for endless possible series of causes and effects, and all thinkable points within it stand for events, each belonging to a thinkable radius. We can tell the distance of any given point from the centre empirically, in virtue of perceiving time, and we can subsequently compare various points if we wish to determine their temporal positions.

If Kant were right, we could discover the distance of points from the centre solely by measuring along a given radius, and we could compare points only if they lay along *one and the same* radius. In fact the circle could have *only one* radius. But Kant is not right. The distances of all possible points from the centre can be compared, and simultaneous events cannot stand as cause and effect to one another. We can see this from the figure, in which simultaneous events must be represented by points lying on the circumference of a smaller circle within the larger, not along *one* radius.

I know that absolute or pure time has only *one* dimension, and that consequently the figure appropriate to it would be a line. But I am not speaking of absolute time. I am speaking of time as possessed of content, and many things have to exist in that simultaneously, owing to the close union of time with space that brings about a totality of experience (a union rather like that of arithmetical multiplication).

It may be noted in passing that the direction of time in the figure of the plane circle may be given its own name: *centripetal*.

Together with Kant's doctrine that objective succession is possible and knowable only through causality goes a parallel doctrine that coexistence is possible and knowable only if there is reciprocity of action (*CPR*, pp. 256-265). This doctrine stands and falls with the first, though it is easier to see through and consequently calls for no separate refutation here. In any event, I fear that my challenge to the first has already become too lengthy.

It is worth adding that even if Kant is wrong in the doctrine that I am challenging, his error has depth, arising as it does from intellectualising the sensibility; and, as an attempt to prove the a priori nature of the law of causality from indisputable facts, it is a brilliant and even blinding piece of theorising.

It is useless trying to defend Kant's doctrine by asserting that he says, not that following upon a cause is the *empirical* criterion of an event's reality and objective position in time, but that it is merely the general condition of the possibility of real succession. It is equally useless to assert that Kant does not say that we must *notice* a causal link before we can recognise a sequence of representations as an event, but only that we must *presuppose* one. Against such assertions I refer to the whole section that I have been challenging: Kant repeats there in a variety of ways that we can only tell an objective from a subjective sequence of representations by recognising the necessity of the way in which it is ordered according to the law of causality, so that it is this ordering that constitutes the criterion for distinguishing the two. And concerning objective coexistence Kant says that 'the coexistence of phenomena not interacting but separated by empty space can never be an object of possible apprehension (pp. 258f.).' (If correct, this would constitute an a priori proof that there is no empty space between the fixed stars.) Or again he says: 'the light *playing be-tween* our eyes and the heavenly bodies brings about an interaction between us and the stars, thus proving the coexistence of the latter (p. 260). (Talk of light *playing between* our eyes and the heavenly bodies introduces the false idea that our eyes affect the light of the stars as well as being affected by it.)

Every *criterion* is empirical, since a criterion is nothing other than a characteristic showing that a single case comes under a rule or concept, and what applies to single cases is always empirical. But if, as suggested in the imagined defence above, we do not need to *notice* but merely to *pre-suppose* the cause of a change in order to recognise its objectivity, the question now inevitably arises, 'How are we to recognise an *alteration* or change of representations as one for which we need to presuppose a cause?' If Kant's meaning is no more than that representations of the class considered in this chapter follow one another and combine in accordance with a law different from that governing concepts and mental images (to be discussed later), so that that law belongs to their *character*, I entirely agree with him. But I do not agree with him if he means that in order to know which class a given set of representations belongs to we need to know which law governing the relevant series of representations is at stake. Just the opposite is true. It is only after we have immediately recognised which class a given set of representations belongs to that we recognise at once and a priori which law governs their sequence and manner of combining. In short, while I agree with Kant that complete representations constituting the totality of experience are causally linked, I deny that knowledge of the objectivity of their sequences is due solely to knowledge of their causal links. For I believe that time is the form not only of representations immediately present to us but of complete representations combined within the totality of experience.

It is with some hesitation that I have ventured to raise these objections to one of Kant's principal doctrines, accepted as proved and repeated even now in the latest publications. For I both admire and revere the depth of Kant's thought, and I owe so much to his teaching that his spirit addresses me in the words of Homer: 'It was I that lifted the mist from your eyes enveloping them before.'[5] But there are sayings from Plato that excuse my having made bold to raise my objections. 'The man is not to be honoured before the truth (*Rep.* X).'[6] And: 'Often those with poor vision see things before those whose vision is sharp (ibid).'[7] Then there are the words of Herder: 'Error wanes: truth remains.'[8]

Finally, if my objections are based upon errors which could mislead others, I hope that what I have written will encourage a clearer exposition of Kant's brilliant doctrine and the discovery of firmer foundations for it.

(This remark is to be taken as applying also to the disagreements with Kant that will be found in Section 26.)

§25 Of the misapplication of the law of causality

The principle of sufficient reason now under consideration holds universally and without limitation within the world of real objects. That is, it holds among complete representations combining to form the total representation of experience. As already sufficiently pointed out, our own body is one of these complete representations, an object among objects, and this means that it is completely subject to the law of causality.

I must assert yet again that the distinction in general between subject and object is the most profound distinction conceivable. Object is whatever is known; subject is whatever knows and, qua knowing, is never known (cf. §42). The relation between subject and object is so necessary that neither is conceivable without it; on the other hand, the principle governing this relation cannot possibly be known, since it is presupposed in knowledge of every sort; knowledge of every sort, being concerned with objects, is only possible given the relation between subject and object.

The laws governing objects are the laws of the faculties of pure sensibility and understanding, proved by Kant to be a priori, and any person taking these laws and applying them to a subject uses them in a transcendent manner and beyond the limits of their validity. For such a person applies laws that are valid for objects of experience to what cannot be an object at all, namely a knowing subject. Nevertheless, not only everyday thought but speculative theorising too has fallen into this error, applying the law of causality to subjects in the way that it is applied to objects, and thereby arriving at two opposing theses and correspondingly opposing systems of thought. According to the first of these, a representation arises from the causal activity of an object, and the subject — playing a passive role — is thus brought under the law of causality. This forms the basis of *realism*. According to the second, a representation arises from the causal activity of a subject, and the subject is again brought under the law of causality — this time playing an active role. This forms the basis of *idealism*.[9]

§26 The time of change

As we have seen, the principle of sufficient reason of becoming applies only to *changes*, and I cannot refrain from making some remarks here, even if they are not entirely in place, about a topic discussed by various philosophers: the time *in which change occurs*.

The views of Plato and Kant particularly are sharply at variance here. Plato asserts that change takes place *suddenly*, occupying *no time at all* (*Parm.*, p. 138).[10] Kant, by contrast, expressly asserts that change does *not take place suddenly*, but *over an interval of time* (*CPR*, p. 253). (Schelling too says something on the topic (*System of Transcendental Idealism*, p. 299), but what he says is so much part of his system of thought that I cannot go into it here. I must content myself with a mere reference to his work.)

I think that I can best bring out my own opinions on the topic by discussing Kant's law of *continuity of change*; what he says on it forms a part of the development of the passage whose reading I recommended above, and is to be found on pages 253-256 of the *Critique of Pure Reason*.

Kant's proof of the continuity of change is in outline as follows. 'As no portion of time is the smallest possible, there is always a time between any two moments, and therefore between any two states occupying time and resulting one from the other. This is *the time in which change takes place*. In it the state that is the cause exerts its influence continuously, the new state emerging gradually and developing through every grade of reality during that time.'

Against this I make two points. The first is that there is no time between two given moments: nor, for that matter, between two given centuries. In time, as in space, there are clear cut boundaries, perceived by us a priori, although we can no more represent such boundaries in time possessed of content than we can represent boundaries in space possessed of content — in which no line can be drawn without breadth. The second point is that time is a continuous quantity, not discrete. Given that empty time could not be apprehended, and that it would abolish the unity of experience if it were, there must be a phenomenon occupying every part of it, so that every series of phenomena constitutes a continuum. In addition, given that every phenomenon consists of objects with changing states, as was brought out above, and indeed changing in such a way that one state always results from another, states likewise must constitute a continuum: that is, every state in time must adjoin the state from which it results without interval. Consequently, owing to the continuum of states, the continuum of time is replete, since if states are to result from one another they can have nothing between them. Contrary to what Kant says, then, there is no such thing as a time in which change takes place, and change is not something existing in time. It is a mere concept employed for the purpose of making comparisons. In other words, it exists purely in thought, as the notion that a state exists now that did not exist before, and that one existed before that does not exist now.

It is important to distinguish discrete from distinct quantity.[11] By a discrete quantity is meant a magnitude whose parts are separated by something *toto genere* different from them, which therefore does not form part of the magnitude. Its opposite is a continuous quantity. By a distinct quantity is meant a magnitude whose parts as such are one in kind but different in species. Its opposite is a univocal quantity.[12]

It is possible for a quantity to be discrete and univocal — for example a row of trees — or continuous and distinct. A series of states is a quantity of the latter kind.

If there existed between any two states what Kant calls a change, something distinct in kind from the states, but like them in occupying time, a series of states would be distinct and discrete, not continuous.[13] But this is not the case. Every series of states is distinct and continuous, distinct in that each state differs in species from the others, continuous in that each state follows another without interval.

The duration of a state is often so brief that we do not apprehend it, owing to the limited acumen of our senses. And between two states possessing sufficient duration for us to apprehend them often lie others that we do not apprehend, the first of which has as its cause the last to be apprehended, while the last has as its effect the first to be apprehended subsequently. We mistakenly think that the last one to be apprehended is the cause of the first to be apprehended subsequently; however, in practice this cannot lead to error, since the last one apprehended is the cause of the states lying between, and is therefore indirectly the cause of the series next to be apprehended.

To think of a time that is filled with states too brief to be apprehended as occupied by something quite different from states, something called a change, conflicts with the law of causality, according to which a state arises only if the one immediately preceding it constitutes its necessary condition. It is precisely on the strength of this that, in cases where a time seems to elapse between cause and effect, we infer the existence of states with duration so brief that each of them escapes empirical notice.

In time, then, there is no such thing as change, there are only states; and, given that states are necessarily juxtaposed without interval, there is no such thing as continuity of change; there is only *continuity of states.* Indeed, this is self-evident, given that change is nothing but a concept arising from reflective acts of comparison, and that continuity does not exist where there is merely a concept, but only where there is a quantity or magnitude in space or time.

That change does not involve duration of time, then, can be proved a priori from the analysis of concepts. But it can also be perceived a priori, though the perception in question is only possible for change constructed out of pure perceptions of space and time: that is, for transition from rest to motion and motion to rest. Given the a priori perceptibility of this kind of change, I can formulate the axiom that between a moment at which a point in space is at rest and a moment at which it moves there cannot be a third at which it is doing neither, but is changing its state.

It would seem, then, that change does not occupy a period of time, although it is only through the notion of time that we have a concept of it; it is for this reason that Plato, whose opinion coincides with this conclusion, says, as I have already pointed out, that the locus of change is 'the sudden' (ἐξαίφνης). This, he says, is 'a thing of peculiar nature, being in no way in time.'[14] He could equally have said simply that its nature is timeless (ἄχρονος φύσις).

There is something just as odd (ἄτοπον) as 'the sudden,' something that also makes sense only in terms of time yet does not occupy time. This is the *present*, the pure dividing line between past and future. Duration is to time what extension is to space; and, just as dividing lines in space are without extension, so is the present without duration. Consequently, it *does not occupy time* and *never* exists. Yet there it is throughout our lives, a fact which explains why we persistently treat it so seriously, even though its contents are for the most part trivial. It explains too why the great insignificance filling most of our lives is accorded a dignity so strange and laughable to reflective persons, on the grounds that it is — *present.* Anyone able to bear this in mind will cease to be laughed at and, like Democritus, will laugh instead.

Perhaps the timelessness of the present, while it makes no sense apart from time, may be explained in the following way. Time is the form of inner sense. Because of this, *every object* must appear in it; by contrast, no *subject* appears in it, because no subject can become object; and the present is the point of contact between subject and object. Further, just as the present is conditioned by time, though itself it is timeless, so time is conditioned by the present. For we have to think of any given time as either past or future, and this means always thinking of it in relation to the present.

Notes

1 κατὰ δύναμιν

2   κατ' ἐντελέχειαν.

3   *Sum, Est.*

4   This can only be properly understood after familiarity with the contents of the following chapter.

5   Ἀχλὺν δ' αὖ τοι ἀπ' ὀφθαλμῶν ἕλον, ἣ πρὶν ἐπῆεν (*Iliad* V, 127).

6   οὐ γάρ πρό γε τῆς ἀληθείας τιμητέος ἀνήρ (*Rep.* 595c2-3).

7   πολλά τοι ὀξύτερον βλεπόντων ἀμβλύτερον ὁρῶντες πρότεροι εἶδον (*Rep.* 595c10-596a1). (Schopenhauer reads πρότερον for πρότεροι (FW).)

8   Der Irrthum schleift sich ab; die Wahrheit bleibet.

9   No advantage is to be gained in the matter considered here by substituting an absolute ego for the subject. For since such an ego is above all else a subject, it cannot come under laws valid for specific classes of objects, since objects exist only with a subject and uniquely for a subject.

10 Stephanus 156c-e (FW).

11 quantum discretum, quantum distinctum.

12 quantum univocum.

13 It would be a discretum distinctum.

14 ἄτοπος φύσις, ἐν χρόνῳ οὐδὲν οὖσα. (A better reading is: φύσις ἄτοπός τις, . . ἐν χρόνῳ οὐδενὶ οὖσα (FW).)

5 On the second class of objects for the subject and the form of the principle of sufficient reason governing it

§27 A statement of this class of objects: reason

The second class of possible objects for the faculty of representation comprises *representations of representations*: in other words, *concepts*. Concepts can be put together to form *judgments*, and judgments in turn to form *syllogisms*. These are formed when through the principle of sufficient reason one judgment is founded entirely upon another or upon two others.

The representations that were considered in the last chapter constitute objects not only for humans but for animals, and they come solely under the faculties of sensibility and understanding.[1] The representations to be considered now, by contrast, are proper to humans, and come under the faculty of *reason*; in other words, *reason is the faculty of representations of representations, the faculty of concepts*. It is important not to confuse concepts with the categories, the operations of the understanding, whose task it is to unite space and time and render them apprehensible. It is particularly important not to confuse them, though this is often done, with the category of unity which unites the manifold of sensuous intuitions.

Sensibility is unable to grasp what causality is, understanding is unable to grasp what temporal sequence and position are, and both are unable to grasp what concepts are. Consequently, it is impossible to have an intuitive representation of the nature of concepts; their nature can only be grasped through concepts themselves. All we can say, then, is that concepts are representations of representations. Further, since reason is the faculty that conjoins concepts, it is also the faculty that conjoins *judgments* into *syllogisms*, in the manner already adverted to. Finally, the presence of representations of this class and the consequent activity of reason upon them is what is meant by 'thought' in the true sense of that word.

I realise that this account of concepts and reason is significantly different from earlier accounts of them, and that the faculties of understanding and reason have never been so sharply divided as they are in this present account of reason and the account of understanding given in Section 19. However, all other accounts I know of strike me as ill defined and inadequate.

The whole of this chapter, in particular Section 33, corroborates my account, and a defence of it is presented in Section 58, the need for such a defence arising from Kant's giving the name of 'practical reason' to something that is not reason at all.

Representations perceived through the immediate object and representations that are repetitions recalled at will, in other words mental images, are both complete and therefore particular. Representations of the two classes yet to be looked at are also particular. *Concepts* by contrast are general. They are nothing other than representations of representations, and consequently cannot contain all that is contained in the representations of which they are representations. In other words, they cannot be completely determinate. However, it is precisely in point of their indeterminacy that they must be representations of many otherwise different representations, and because of this that they possess a general sphere of application.

What makes the preservation and communication of concepts possible is language, since without language concepts would not be fixed. But language in turn is impossible without concepts, since it is a tool of concepts and nothing else.

Proper names constitute an exception, and do not really belong to language, since they do not refer to concepts but directly to particulars. That is why animals easily understand them.

§28 Uses of concepts

However, for the very reason that concepts contain less than the representations of which they are representations, they are easier to handle. They stand to their respective representations rather as formulae in arithmetic stand to the mental processes from which they are derived and for which they are substitutes, and they preserve only those elements of representations that are useful. If we used our imagination to recall the representations themselves, we should be obliged as it were to drag around an enormous burden of inessentials, and would consequently be easily confused. As it is, we recall only those elements and relationships of representations that our purposes and circumstances require. It is for this reason that concepts are the essential material of the sciences, since the aim of these is ultimately to acquire knowledge of the particular through the general. This is only possible through the principle of *dictum de omni et nullo*,[2] and this in turn is only possible through the availability of concepts.

§29 Representatives of concepts

As was said earlier, mental images should not be confused with concepts. Although they are not produced through the immediate object and do not belong to the totality of experience, mental images are complete, particular representations, and are therefore to be distinguished from concepts, even in cases where they are used *to stand for concepts*. This happens when we would like to have the representations themselves before us, matching the concepts of which they are representations. But such a wish cannot be fulfilled since, to illustrate the point, there is no such thing as a representation or matching mental image of a dog simply as such, nor of a colour, triangle or number as such. In cases of this sort we conjure up a mental image of, say, a particular dog, and given that this mental image is a representation, it is necessarily determinate in all respects. It has determinate size, colour and shape, even though the concept it represents has none of these. However, when using substitutes for concepts in this way, we are conscious that they do not match their concepts adequately but are full of arbitrary determinations.

(For what concerns Platonic Ideas, see note to Section 40.)

What has been said here is in obvious conflict with what Kant says in his chapter on schematism (*CPR*, pp. 176-181), and only introspection and clear reflection can settle the issue. Let us investigate, then, if in the case of a concept we are aware of a 'monogram of the pure a priori imagination.' To take an example, let us see if when we focus on the concept of dog we are conscious of something *entre chien et loup*, or if, on the contrary and in keeping with what has been said here, one of two things occurs: reason presents us with a concept, or imagination presents us with a substitute for a concept in the form of a complete picture.

§30 Truth

The sole use of concepts is in judgments, and judgments are without value unless they are *true*.

To say that a judgment is *true* is to say that there exists a sufficient reason for it, distinct from the judgment itself. *Consequently, truth is a relation between a judgment and something beyond it.*

§31 The principle of sufficient reason of knowing

It follows from what has been said that our principle appears here as *the principle of sufficient reason of knowing*, principium rationis sufficientis cognoscendi, and it is named in this way because it is a guiding thread that leads us to knowledge.

A *judgment* without a reason is not true, has no source in knowledge. As was said a moment ago, truth is a relation between a judgment and something beyond it, and upon which it can lean or rest, and the German word for reason, *Grund*, is therefore well chosen. However, there are four kinds of reason that judgments can rest upon, and the kinds of truth that they acquire vary accordingly. These different kinds will be set out in the following four sections.

§32 Logical truth

One judgment can be based upon another as its reason, and in such a case its truth is *logical* or *formal*. Whether or not it possesses material truth as well is not *eo ipso* decided: it does if it rests upon a judgment possessing material truth, or if this last judgment in turn rests upon a series of judgments that rest upon a judgment possessing material truth. This dependence of judgments upon others is always due to the subsumption of concepts under concepts, and the form of a *syllogism* shows up when this is clearly pictured. Syllogisms are constituted by judgments resting upon other judgments, and therefore have to do with nothing but judgments. Judgments in turn are merely conjunctions of concepts, and, since concepts are the exclusive domain of reason, syllogistic inference is correctly said to be the proper concern of reason.

The truth of some judgments is evident from a consideration of the four well known basic principles of thought, and I hold that each of these judgments rests upon another, this other being one of the basic principles of thought underlying its truth. For example, the judgment, 'A triangle is a space enclosed by three lines,' has the principle of identity for its ultimate reason; 'No body is without extension,' the principle of contradiction; 'Every judgment is true or not true,' the principle of excluded middle. Finally, 'No one can accept something as true without knowing why,' has the principle of sufficient reason of knowing for its final reason. In the ordinary course of reasoning, people assume the truth of judgments following from these abstract basic principles of thought without appealing to them as premises; indeed most people have not even heard of them. But the judgments in question are not thereby rendered independent of those principles as premises, any more than the judgment, 'This body will fall if you take away its support,' is rendered independent of the judgment, 'All bodies tend towards the middle of the earth,' on the grounds that the latter may never have entered the consciousness of this or that person making it.

Because of this, I cannot approve of logicians' hitherto ascribing *intrinsic truth* to judgments supported by nothing other than the laws of thought, declaring them to be *immediately true*. For this is to distinguish *intrinsic logical truth* from *extrinsic logical truth*, the latter being the dependence of one judgment upon another as its reason; but since every truth is a relation between a judgment and something *beyond* it, the notion of *intrinsic truth* is incoherent.

§33 Empirical truth

A judgment possesses *material* truth if it has experience as its reason, and it possesses *empirical truth* if it rests upon experience *immediately*.

To say that a judgment has *material* truth means in general that its concepts are conjoined and qualified in such a way that they correspond to how the representations of which they are themselves representations are conjoined in experience and qualified in relation to the totality to which they belong. It follows that concepts must have as many ways of being conjoined and qualified as do representations constituting the totality of experience.

39

It is here that we discover the real reason behind the fact that nothing but the *table of judgments* could furnish a true guide to the discovery of the *categories*. Every operation of the understanding in conjoining representations to form a whole of experience must be matched by a way of conjoining concepts, the representations of representations just referred to; and it is surely in virtue of this that we possess reason. For reason is not the faculty concerned with complete representations and with conjoining these to make up the whole of experience. In other words, it is not the faculty that we share with animals, but a higher ability, so to speak: a faculty of representations of complete representations, capable moreover of conjoining these in a manner corresponding to the ways in which complete representations themselves are conjoined. In short, we possess a faculty of concepts and judgments which is not shared by animals.

It follows that general logic stands in the same relation to reason as transcendental logic to the understanding, and has therefore very properly been called the theory of reasoning. The forms of general logic ought therefore to provide a guide to discovering the forms of transcendental logic, though strictly speaking only in so far as general logic treats of possible connections and relations that concepts have to one another in judgments, and of possible connections that categorical judgments have to one another when conjoined to constitute hypothetical or disjunctive judgments. This examination of possible connections by general logic corresponds to the examination by transcendental logic of possible connections among the forms of sensibility that are rendered apprehensible by the categories. In what concerns *syllogisms*, however, it is the judgments *themselves* that constitute the object of investigation under the principle of sufficient reason (the universal principle of dependency), not merely the representations whose representations the concepts contained in the judgments are. Consequently, syllogisms are not related to the understanding or to transcendental logic; they are exclusively the domain of reason and general logic.

As the faculty of concepts and judgments in general, reason must be as Kant has described it: the faculty of a priori principles. For principles can only be established in abstract form, and therefore only through reason, even when their origin lies in the understanding or sensibility. It was no doubt Kant's establishing of this characteristic of reason that led him to think of even the moral law as based upon reason — named 'practical' for the purpose. On the grounds that this law is not derivable from experience, he considered that it must be an a priori principle, ignoring the fact that knowledge of what *must* be and cannot be otherwise is *toto coelo* different from knowledge of what *ought* to be.

(It is the above ability of reason to establish abstract a priori principles and to make inferences, together with the fact that unlike the understanding it is not directly bound to sensibility, that leads it to what Kant called its *ideas*. It leads in this direction because, starting out from metaphysical principles and influenced by the faculty of pure sensibility which goes on to infinity, it continues making its inferences; while at the same time, influenced by the faculty of the understanding which brings unity and creates the totality of experience, it seeks totality and completeness in the series of inferences that it pursues.)

Reason then is the faculty now clearly described, nothing else. It not only renders science possible, but in addition possesses the incomparable value of enabling us to *guide our behaviour through concepts*, instead of acting under the exclusive influence of *particular representations* — as is the case with animals. Consequently, actions are said to be *rational* if they are guided by concepts and are not the results of the particular representations that chance to be before the mind; they are independent of these. The possibility of such actions is a precondition of freedom; and animals, not possessing concepts, are consequently at the mercy of their immediate desires or emotions. In our case, by contrast, however much the presence of representations may alter and seek to solicit our wills, our *concepts remain fast*. Furthermore, in enabling us through concepts to look at the whole of our lives with all their events, reason constitutes the condition of that equanimity and steadfastness with which the accidents and trials of life are accepted by those commonly referred to as practical philosophers, though that name implies no moral standing arising from such steadfastness. Finally, reason and concepts constitute the conditions of all reflective, thought-out and premeditated activity, of all so called great deeds and misdeeds. In virtue of these many ways in which it is connected with our behaviour, reason may properly be spoken of as *practical*, though not in the sense of that word introduced by Kant and still universally prevailing. (A fuller account of this will be found in §58.)

§34 Metaphysical truth

There are some judgments whose reason is constituted by the conditions of all experience, and these are both synthetic a priori and possessed of material, in fact *metaphysical*, truth. The explanation of this is that what determines them is precisely what determines experience itself: namely, either the forms of pure sensibility, objects of a priori perception, or the categories of the understanding, objects of a priori knowledge.

The following are examples of judgments of this kind. 'Two straight lines cannot enclose a space.' 'Nothing happens without a cause.' '3 x 7 = 21.' 'There is no middle state between rest and motion.'

§35 Metalogical truth

Finally, there are judgments whose reason is constituted by the conditions of all thought; and in order to describe the truth of these, I feel obliged to introduce a new word, speaking of *metalogical truth*. There are only four judgments of this kind, long ago discovered inductively and declared to be the basic principles of thought. Further, there is agreement over what in general they signify, even if there has never been unanimity concerning their formulation and number. The four are as follows. 'A subject is equal to the sum of its properties, $a = a$.' 'No subject possesses a property that is contradictory to it; $a = \sim a = 0$.' 'All subjects must possess one of any pair of contradictory properties.' 'Truth is the relation of a judgment to something beyond it.' This last is the principle of sufficient reason of knowing.

That these judgments are expressions of the conditions of all thought, and consequently have these as their reason, is known to us by means of a kind of reflection that I will call reason's self-investigation. What I have in mind is that reason discovers that these laws are the conditions

41

of the possibility of thought by making vain attempts to think contrary to them; just as experimentation discovers what movements our bodies can make — in precisely the same way indeed as it discovers the characteristics of all other objects. By contrast, if as subjects we were able to know ourselves, we would be able to recognise these laws *directly*, rather than through experiments on objects — that is, on representations. The same holds good of the reasons of judgments possessing metaphysical truth. These too cannot come before our consciousness directly, but must first be presented *in concreto* through the intermediary of objects — that is, through the intermediary of representations.

There is in general a great and noticeable similarity and relationship between metaphysical truth and metalogical truth, a fact that points to their having a common root. In this chapter the principle of sufficient reason appears particularly as a metalogical truth; in the last chapter it appeared as a metaphysical truth; in the next it will again appear as metaphysical, though under a different form. Because of this I am at pains in this dissertation to present the principle of sufficient reason as a judgment having a fourfold reason, not four different reasons leading accidentally to the same judgment. There is but a single judgment, appearing as fourfold, which by way of imagery I call a fourfold root.

The first three metalogical truths listed above are so alike that in treating of them one feels almost obliged to seek a common expression for them; the fourth, by contrast, the principle of sufficient reason, is clearly distinct.

If we wanted a metaphysical analogue for the three, the best choice would be the metaphysical truth that substance perdures.

NOTE. It should be noted that the relation of a reason of knowing to a consequent gives rise to a hypothetical judgment only in those cases where the reason is itself a judgment. This point is implicit in the concept of a hypothetical judgment, since a hypothetical judgment is one that combines two judgments in the relation of reason to consequent.

Notes

1   Needless to say, the understanding possessed by animals is duller than that possessed by humans, while at all sorts of levels the senses of animals are sharper. Likewise, the understanding possessed by men is found to be duller here, sharper there; just like the senses. Someone having a clearer and more general grasp of the connections and relations among things is one who possesses sharper understanding, and such a one is consequently in a position to apply his reason to more complex combinations of concepts.

2   The principle that whatever is affirmed or denied of an entire class or kind may be affirmed or denied of any part (FW).

6 On the third class of objects for the subject and the form of the principle of sufficient reason governing it

§36 Statement of this class of objects

The third class of objects for the faculty of representation is constituted by the formal element of those representations that are complete: that is, it is constituted by the a priori perceptions of space and time, the forms of outer and inner sense.

As pure perceptions, these objects for the faculty of representation are absolute. That is, they are distinct from complete representations and from the characteristic of having or not having content, which comes only with complete representations. For not even pure points and lines can be represented visually: they can only be perceived a priori, just as the infinite extent and divisibility of space and time can only be objects of pure, not empirical, perception.

In these respects, space and time contrast with the conditions of a total representation of experience. For these conditions — the categories — which lie within the understanding, are not absolute and distinct objects for the faculty of representation. On the contrary, they are to be found only in those representations whose condition they are — that is, only *in concreto*. Consequently, it is only through abstraction that a concept of them, a representation of a representation of them, can be formed. A representation of them *tout simple* is impossible.

§37 The principle of reason of being

Space and time are characterised by the fact that their parts are all interrelated and consequently determined and conditioned by one another, the relevant relation in space being *position*, in time *succession*. These relations are peculiar to space and time, and entirely different from all other possible relations among representations. They can therefore be apprehended only by perception, not by the understanding, since there is no way in which the understanding can grasp relations such as above and below, right and left, behind and in front, before and after.

The law in accordance with which parts of space and time determine one another, related in the ways mentioned above, I call *the principle of sufficient reason of being*, principium rationis sufficientis essendi. In Section 14 the connection between sides and angles of a triangle has already been cited as an illustration of this law, where it was made clear that the relation in question is totally different from that of cause and effect or reason of knowing and consequent, so that here the condition may properly be termed reason of *being*, ratio essendi.

It goes without saying that a grasp of a *reason of being* can become a reason of knowing, just as a grasp of the law of causality and its application in a given case can become a reason of knowing in respect of the relevant effect. But this in no way destroys the distinction between reasons of being, becoming and knowing.

I turn now to a general and abstract exposition of this law.

§38 Reason of being in space

In space, the position of any given part relative to a second, for example the position of a given line (area, body, or point) relative to a second, completely determines its position relative to a possible third, so that the second position in relation to the first stands as consequent to reason. And, since the position of the given line relative to any possible other determines its position relative to all positions, including that referred to a moment ago as determined in relation to the first, it is a matter of indifference which is seen as determined by the others — in other words, which position is seen as the reason (*ratio*) on which the others are based (*rationata*). The explanation of this is that there is no succession in space, and the explanation of this in turn is that it is only through the union of space and time resulting in the totality of experience that the representation of coexistence arises. Consequently, all reasons of being in space have a characteristic analogous to the relation of interaction, of which I shall treat in greater detail in Section 54 when I consider the reciprocity of reasons.

Since in respect of position any given line is determined by others as much as it determines them, it is a matter of pure choice whether we view it as determined or determining. Further, the position of one line relative to a second allows of a question concerning its position relative to a third — a second position which necessitates the first. Consequently, in any series of reasons of being, as in any series of reasons of becoming, no terminus is to be found in the antecedent part of the series (*a parte priori*);

44

nor, because of the infinity of space and the number of possible lines within it, in the succeeding part (*a parte posteriori*).

All possible relative spaces are figures, because they have boundaries. Moreover, given that they possess common boundaries, they have their reasons of being in one another. In space, a series of reasons of being (*series rationum essendi*) proceeds to infinity (*in indefinitum*), just as does a series of reasons of becoming (*series rationum fiendi*); indeed, unlike the latter, it proceeds not in one direction but in all.

It is impossible to prove these assertions, since their truth is metaphysical, based directly upon our a priori perception of space.

§39 Reason of being in time: arithmetic

Every moment of time is conditioned by its predecessor, and the reason of being here — the law of succession — is simple. This is because time is unidimensional and incapable therefore of a diversity of relations. Every moment is conditioned by its predecessor and can only be reached through its predecessor. In other words, only in virtue of the fact that one moment *has existed* and passed away does another *now exist*.

All counting, the whole of arithmetic therefore, rests on this connectedness of parts of time. Every number presupposes its predecessors as the reasons of its being: I can only reach ten through the numbers preceding it, and only by grasping the relevant reason of being do I know that where there is ten there is eight, six and four.

§40 Geometry

In the same way, the whole of geometry rests upon the interconnectedness of the positions possessed by parts of space; and, if properly pursued, geometry would be an intellectual grasp of that interconnectedness. Further, given that this grasp is not possible through the understanding, as was said earlier, but only through perception, all geometrical propositions would be founded upon perception, geometrical proofs properly consisting solely in bringing out the relevant connections to be perceived. There is nothing more that they could achieve. However, the way in which geometry is in fact pursued is very different. Only Euclid's twelve axioms are held to rest upon perception; and of these only the ninth, eleventh and twelfth rest upon genuinely independent perceptions. The others are taken to rest upon the insight that science, unlike experience, does not deal with complete representations, existing independently and side by side in endless possible variety, but with concepts and — in mathematics — with *ideal particulars* (Normalanschauungen),[1] in other words with figures and numbers. These ideal particulars have universal application to the totality of experience, and are consequently able to combine the comprehensiveness of concepts with the complete determinateness of individual representations. As genuine representations they are fully determinate, and *as such* leave no room for the generality of indeterminacy; at the same time, however, they are general in that they are the bare forms of all phenomena, and as such have application to all real objects to which these forms belong. Consequently, what Plato says of his Ideas

45

would hold of ideal particulars — even in geometry — as it does of concepts: namely, that no two can exist that are alike, since any such two would be but one.[2] This assertion would hold of ideal particulars in geometry as elsewhere, I say, were it not for the fact that these purely *spatial* objects are distinct from one another simply in being *juxtaposed*, in having position.

Now it seems to me that a simple grasp of the fact that difference of position does not affect identity in other respects could stand in the place of the above axioms. Further, this substitution would better accord with the nature of science, since the goal of science is to acquire knowledge of the particular through the general. What I mean is that this substitution would better accord with the nature of science than the enunciation of nine different axioms all based upon a single insight.

In the case of the ideal particulars of time, numbers, there is not even such a difference as juxtaposition; rather, as in the case of concepts, there is nothing but the identity of indiscernibles (*identitas indiscernibilium*), and there is only one number five and one seven. Indeed, in this may be found a reason for saying that the proposition, '7 + 5 = 12,' is not one of identity, *pace* Herder in his *Metacritique*. The proposition, '12 = 12,' is a proposition of identity, but the proposition, '7 + 5 = 12,' is synthetic a priori and based upon pure perception, as we know from Kant's penetrating insights.

In geometry, then, only in the case of the axioms is appeal genuinely made to perception. The theorems are demonstrated — that is, based upon reasons of knowing obliging us to accept their truth. Consequently, they provide us with logical reasons, not with the relevant metaphysical reasons. But metaphysical reasons, since they are reasons of *being*, not *knowing*, only become evident through perception (§§32, 34), and because of this we are convinced after a demonstration that the demonstrated proposition is true, but we do not see why it is true. This means that we have not grasped the relevant reason of being, and in fact it is usually only at this point that we desire to do so. For, a proof that consists in providing a reason of knowing brings conviction (*convictio*) but not insight (*cognitio*), and is perhaps more correctly called a refutation (*elenchus*) than a demonstration (*demonstratio*).[3] Because of this, geometrical proof usually leaves us with the sort of unpleasant feeling that is always produced when we realise that we cannot see why something is so; and in this case we only perceive our failure to see *why* something is so when we are provided with the knowledge *that it is so*. By contrast, a reason of being of a proposition in geometry, apprehended through perception, brings satisfaction, as does every acquisition of knowledge. Once we apprehend it, we base our conviction of the truth of the relevant proposition upon it, and from then on cease to rely on the reason of knowing provided in the demonstration.

This point may be illustrated from the sixth proposition of Euclid's first book: 'If two angles of a triangle are equal, the sides opposite them are equal too.' Euclid proves this in the following way.

Let *abg* be a triangle having the angle *abg* equal to the angle *agb*. I assert that the side *ag* must likewise be equal to the side *ab*. For if side *ag* is not equal to side *ab*, one of the two is greater. Let *ab* be the greater. From this greater *ab* a segment *db* is cut off, equal to the

46

smaller *ag*, and the line *dg* is drawn. Given that now, in the triangles *dbg, abg, db* is equal to *ag*, while *bg* is common to both, it follows that the two sides *db* and *bg* are equal to the sides *ag, gb* respectively, the angle *dbg* is equal to the angle *agb*, the base *dg* equal to the base *ab*, and the triangle *abg* is equal to the triangle *dgb*, the greater to the smaller, which is nonsense. It follows that *ab* is not unequal to *ag*, and so is equal to it.

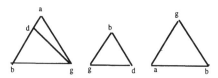

Figure 1

In this proof we are furnished with a reason of knowing for the truth of the theorem. But who bases his conviction upon this proof of the geometrical truth? Who does not rather base it upon the reason of being that is recognised through perception and which guarantees — in virtue of a necessity that cannot be further demonstrated but can only be perceived — that if from the end points of a line two further lines are drawn inclining equally towards each other, these can only meet at a point equidistant from the end points? Because the two resulting angles are really one, only seeming to be two because they are positioned opposite to each other, there is no reason why the lines should meet closer to one end point than another.

Through knowledge of the reason of being we grasp the relation of necessary consequence between something conditioned and its condition (in this case, between the equality of the sides and the equality of the angles): we see the connectedness of the two, whereas through the reason of knowing we are aware only of their coexistence. It may even be said that the usual method of proof merely convinces us that there is coexistence in the particular figure given as an example, certainly not in all cases. Consequently, given that we are not shown the necessity of the relevant connection, we acquire the conviction of coexistence merely through induction, based upon the fact that we notice coexistence in all figures of the kind drawn.

It must be conceded that it is only in simple theorems like Euclid's sixth just presented that reasons of being are so plain to see. I am none the less convinced that even in the most complicated theorem it must be possible to show the relevant reason of being, bringing out that the truth of the theorem rests upon simple perception. In fact, we all have clear a priori awareness that there must be a reason of being for any spatial relation, just as that there must be a cause for any change. All the same, it is difficult to show the reason of being in a complicated theorem, and in any event this is no place for advanced investigations into geometry.

Simply to make my meaning clearer, I will take a proposition only moderately more complicated than Euclid's sixth, but whose reason of being is not immediately obvious, and I will try to show how it can be traced back to a reason of being. Passing over ten theorems, I come to the six-teenth: 'In every triangle of which one side has been produced, the exterior angle is greater than either of the interior opposite angles.' Euclid's proof goes as follows.

Let the triangle be *abg* and let the side *bg* be produced to *d*. I maintain that the exterior angle *agd* is greater than either of the opposite interior angles. Let the side *ag* be bisected at *e*; let *be* be drawn and then produced to *z* in such a way that *ez* is equal to *eb*; let *zg* be joined and *ag* be produced to *h*.

Now because *ae* is equal to *eg* and *be* to *ez*, the two sides *ae* and *eb* are equal to *ge* and *ez* respectively, and the angle *aeb* equal to *zeg*, given that they are vertical and opposite angles. It follows that the base *a b* is equal to the base *zg*, the triangle *abe* equal to the triangle *zeg*, and the remaining angles equal to the remaining angles, and consequently that the angle *bae* is equal to the angle *egz*. But the angle *egd* is greater than *egz*, as a result of which the angle *agd* is also greater than the angle *bae*.

Let *bg* be bisected, and it will be proved in similar fashion that the angle *bgh* — that is, its vertical and opposite angle *agd* — is greater than *abg*.

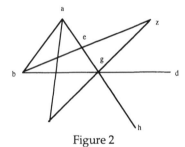

Figure 2

I would prove the same proposition in the following way.

For angle *bag* to be equal to angle *agd*, let alone greater than it, line *b a* that meets with *ga* would have to lie in the same direction as *bd* (this being precisely what is meant by equality of angles). That is, *ba* would have to be parallel to *bd*; in other words, it could never meet it. However, if a triangle is to be formed, *ba* must (reason of being) meet *bd*, and so bring about the opposite of what would be required for angle *bag* to be even the same size as *agd*.

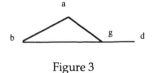

Figure 3

For angle *abg* to be equal to angle *agd*, let alone greater than it, line *ba* would have to lie in the same direction towards *bd* as *ag* (this being precisely what is meant by equality of angles). That is, it would have to be parallel to *ag*; in other words, it could never meet it. However, if a triangle is to be formed, it must meet *ag*, and so bring about the opposite of what would be required for angle *abg* to be even the same size as *agd*.

I do not wish to propose a new method of mathematical demonstration here, nor do I wish to replace Euclid's proof with my own; the entire nature of my proof makes it unsuitable for such a role, as does the fact that it presupposes the concept of parallel lines which appears only later in Euclid. I simply wish to bring out what reasons of being are, and to make clear how different they are from reasons of knowing, which produce nothing but conviction — something very different from insight into reasons of being.

Geometry aims at producing mere conviction, and because of this leaves behind it the sort of disagreeable impression I mentioned earlier. It does not aim at producing insight into reasons of being, generating the feelings of satisfaction and pleasure that insight characteristically engenders. This may be one of the reasons why so many otherwise good minds dislike mathematics.

Notes

1   To translate *Normalanschauungen* by *normal perceptions* might mislead the reader. While Normalanschauungen means literally normal perceptions or intuitions, it seems fairly plain that what Schopenhauer has in mind is that a circle, say, as apprehended in pure intuition is a particular which stands for or represents circles in general; it is something like a 'mathematical' of the kind attributed by Aristotle to Plato (*Metaphysics*, I, 6). Cf. *World as Will and Representation* II, Chapter XIII, and see Kant, *CPR*, Transcendental Doctrine of Method, Chapter 1, Section 1. (FW.)

2   *Platonic Ideas* may perhaps be described as ideal particulars which, unlike those that are mathematical, hold not only of the formal constituents of complete representations but of their material constituents too. In this case they would be complete representations, and as such they would be totally determinate yet at the same time, like concepts, would embrace a great deal within them. That is, in keeping with what I explained in Section 29, they would be representatives of concepts, though fully adequate as such.

3   When Socrates engaged in discussion with his interlocutors, his aim was a refutation — an ἔλεγχος — of their claims to knowledge and understanding; he aimed to convince them that while they thought they understood this or that, they understood nothing. Schopenhauer's wry suggestion is that, rather than getting us to 'see' this or that geometrical truth, as it should, a Euclidean proof merely succeeds in convincing us that we understand nothing. In that sense it constitutes a refutation. It produces a numbness in us similar to that produced by the sting of an electric torpedo fish (*Meno* 80). (FW.)

7 On the fourth class of objects for the subject and the form of the principle of sufficient reason governing it

§41 General statement

The last class of objects for the faculty of representation remaining to be considered comprises only *one* object, namely the immediate object of our inner sense: in other words, *the subject of the will.*

This subject of the will constituting an object for the knowing subject is given solely to the inner sense, as a result of which it appears only in time, not in space; and even in time with one important qualification.

§42 Subject of knowing and object

When a subject is *known*, it is known only as something that *wills*, as a source of spontaneous activity: it is not known as something that *knows*. This is because the representing 'I,' in other words the subject of knowing, is a necessary correlate and therefore condition of all representations, so that it cannot itself become a representation or object. *It is for this reason that it is impossible to have knowledge of knowledge*, as may be brought out by the following considerations. Whenever an instance of knowledge arises, it produces a synthetic proposition, whether a priori or a posteriori. *But the proposition 'I know' is analytic*, since knowing is an inseparable property of 'I' — the subject of knowing and judging — and is always presupposed in conjunction with it. And in fact the subject of the analytic proposition, 'I know,' is not a result of synthesis, but is in the strictest sense 'original,' being given as the condition of all representations. To be a subject is simply to know, to be an object is simply to be known, from which it follows that knowing cannot itself be known, since this would require a subject to separate itself from its knowing in order to know that knowing. Such a separation is impossible, not only because it is contradictory, but because the whole essence of a subject qua subject is to know, so that it cannot be thought of as separate from its knowing.

To this you might make the following objection. 'I do not merely know. I know that I know.' I should reply that your awareness that you know is only verbally distinguishable from your knowing. For, 'I know that I know' says no more than 'I know,' and this, without further qualification, says no more than 'I.' If you still believe that your knowing and your awareness of knowing are different, try thinking of each as existing on its own. Try to know without being aware that you are knowing, and try to be aware of knowing without your awareness itself being knowing.

It is of course possible to abstract from all *specific* cases of knowing, and in this way to arrive at the proposition, 'I know,' the ultimate possible abstraction. But this 'I know' is identical with 'There are objects for me,' and this is identical with 'I am a subject,' which in turn is no more than 'I.'

Someone might ask the following question. If the subject is not known, how is it that its various cognitive faculties are known, the faculties of sensibility, understanding and reason? The answer is that these are not known as a result of knowing's becoming an object for us; were this so, there would be fewer contradictory judgments about our faculties. Rather, they are inferred; or, more correctly, they are general expressions for the classes of representations that have been established and which are at all times more or less precisely distinguished in these very cognitive faculties. But when we are thinking of the subject itself, that is, the necessary condition and correlate of representations, the cognitive faculties are considered in abstraction from representations, and are consequently related to the classes of representations in the way that a subject is to its object when subject and object are considered abstractly. The object is posited together with its subject (the very word 'object' being otherwise devoid of meaning), the subject with its object. Consequently, to be a subject means to have an object; to be an object means to be known by a subject. *Pari passu*, if an object is posited as *determined in a particular way*, the subject is posited as *knowing in that particular way*. It follows that it is a matter of indifference whether I say, 'Objects possess such and such determinations proper to them,' or I say, 'The subject knows in such and such ways.' It is a matter of indifference whether I say, 'Objects are to be assigned to such and such classes,' or I say, 'Such and such distinct cognitive faculties belong to the subject.'

If the identity of subjective and objective that the philosophy of nature (Naturphilosophie) asserts means nothing more than this indifference, I completely agree with it. But I doubt that this is all it means, since no intellectual intuition is required to arrive at such a conclusion; one needs no more than thought. If, therefore, someone wishes to call two things one because neither of them can be thought without the other, I have no objection to this. 'Provided that what is at issue is understood, let us not be over nice in our use of words.'¹ None the less, what in fact is involved is a single necessary relation, a single property possessed by two relata; I allow of nothing else. In any event, there are other pairs whose

51

members stand in exactly the same relation: for example, cause and effect, father and son, brother and sister. *Taken as such*, the members of these pairs can only be thought together, each member having significance only through the other; yet they are not for this reason said to be one, but two. (It should be noted, however, that whenever the pairs just mentioned exist *in concreto*, they possess other properties as well.)

In brief, it is all one whether we say, 'Sensibility and understanding are no more,' or we say, 'The world is at an end.' It is all one whether we say, 'There are no concepts,' or we say, 'Reason has gone, and only animals now exist.'

It is worth noting that failure in the past to appreciate this relation between subject and object gave rise to two major disputes — still perhaps unresolved, and capable of resolution only if the nature of the relation is grasped. The first was that between the old dogmatic philosophers and the Kantians. In other words, it was a dispute between ontology and metaphysics on the one hand and transcendental aesthetic and logic on the other. The origin of it was a failure to understand the relation with respect to the first and third classes of representations that I have established. The second dispute, throughout the whole of the middle ages, was that between realists and nominalists, and its origin was a failure to appreciate the importance of the relation with respect to the second class of representations.

What happens if all *ways* and all *determinations* of being an object are *thought away*, together therefore with all ways and determinations of knowing or being a subject? I am not asking what happens if these are *abstracted* from, which is to think away their differences and so to come to the general concepts of object and subject. What I am asking is what happens if all ways of being and all determinations are *thought away*, so that only object and subject remain to be thought (a process that cannot be completed, only attempted). The answer is that all determinate cognitive faculties vanish, and correspondingly all determinate classes of representations. But something still remains on either side: an x and a y. In other words, something remains that is neither time nor space, nor the understanding which binds these together, nor *a fortiori* the faculty of reason presupposing them and their interrelations. What remains is what is presupposed in the outline I gave of the analysis of experience: on the side of the object what remains is matter, the apprehensibility of the forms referred to above; on the other side what remains is what does the apprehending, the knowing *subject, indeterminate in its manner* of knowing. As was observed, this kind of 'thinking away' can never be completed, since in thought space always accompanies matter, and time the knowing subject.

That what remains is an x and a y is due to the fact that the first is too dark to be known, so to speak, the other too bright. However, the following at least is plain. Our investigation does not freeze in a thing in itself, since even the x and the y — just like their determinations and forms now thought away — can only be thought of in relation to each another; given this relationship they have significance, without it they disappear. If, then, on these grounds there are some who wish to call them one, I shall concur, though only given the explanation and qualification that I put forward earlier.

If we intuited an absolute identity between subject and object, bringing them under the category of unity, we should gain the advantage of having one unknown quantity instead of two. However, we do not have such an intuition. Moreover, given that the category of unity, like the other categories, cannot be applied to what is not an object, what in the end we are confronted with is the phenomenon of consciousness appearing as subject and object, reduced to its original bareness, imperfectly apprehensible and eluding all attempts at definition.

If you ask, 'Why is there this appearance of subject and object at all?' my answer for the moment is that your very question presupposes subject and object — and even their forms and laws — just as does the principle of sufficient reason from which it derives its sole authority. But I suspect that from an area of philosophy very different from that of my present treatise we may well receive not so much an answer to this question as something rendering it superfluous and satisfying us in a very different manner.

A short while ago we looked at disputes arising from failure to grasp the true relation between determinate subjects on the one hand — made determinate through sensibility, understanding and reason — and determinate objects on the other hand, corresponding to such subjects. In like fashion, failure to appreciate the relation now sketched out between subject and object devoid of determinations was the original source of idealism and realism, the first of which imagines itself able to conceive of subjects without objects, the second to conceive of objects without subjects.

§43 Subject of willing

We see, then, that the subject of knowing can itself never be known, can never be an object or representation, since the *proposition, 'I know,' is analytic.* '*I will*,' by contrast, is *synthetic*; indeed it is given to us a posteriori through experience, in this case through inner experience, that is, solely in time, though in everyone's consciousness it is most probably the first empirical proposition and the one with which our knowledge begins. To this extent, the subject of willing may be said to be an object for us.

None the less, the identity of the subject of willing with the subject of knowing, in virtue of which and necessarily the word 'I' includes and denotes both, is altogether beyond comprehension. For only relations among objects come within the scope of comprehension, and any given two of these can only be one in virtue of being parts of a single whole. Here, where the subject is in question, the rules governing knowledge of objects are no longer applicable, and the real identity between knower and that which as willing is known — that is, between subject and object — is *given directly*. Whoever has a true conception of the incomprehensibility of this identity will call it, as I do, the miracle of miracles.

§44 Willing

It is precisely because the subject of willing is given directly to our inner sense that the nature of *willing* itself allows of no further definition or description. It is of course possible to point to certain characteristics, such as change and causality, that it shares with other states; and, since it is from these other states that the characteristics of willing are known in the first instance, it is they that enable it thus far to be thought of. By contrast, there is no corresponding way in which its essential nature is revealed, and because of this it cannot be brought under further concepts. It follows that we may, and even must, simply presuppose that we know what willing is.

For the sake of a more effective set of distinctions, I wish to mention a few of the states related to willing but not to be confused with it. *Acting* is not willing, but the effect brought about by willing when this becomes causal. To say that I *can* do such and such an action is to say that the external conditions are satisfied for the willing of it to become causal. What is called *desire* is willing as long as this does not become causal but continues to be thwarted, either by external conditions or by some other instance of willing within the same subject. When desires conflict, the one that becomes causal is said to be willing in the fullest sense of the word and by contrast with the others.[2] What is called a *decision* is an act through which causality is imparted to a desire, if not straight away and actually (κατ᾽ ἐντελέχειαν), at least potentially (κατὰ δύναμιν). Desires conflicting with another desire that is raised to the status of willing continue as desires; and, if morally superior to it, they are commonly referred to as *good desires* — a way of wording the rebuke that what ought to have become willing remained desire, and that what ought to have remained desire became willing.

§45 Law of motivation

Considered from the point of view of what comes after it (*a parte posteriori*) willing falls under the law of causality, since it is causally active in respect of real objects, including the immediate object of both knowing and willing, the body. But under what law does it fall when considered from the point of view of what precedes it (*a parte priori*)? Does every instance of willing follow a preceding state in accordance with a rule, that is necessarily? Or is willing a faculty capable of initiating series of states on its own? This is the ancient debate about freedom.

With every decision that we become aware of, our own or another's, we consider ourselves justified in asking 'Why?' In other words, we presuppose that every decision is necessarily preceded by something from which it results. On the other hand, we always have a strong, often even disquieting, consciousness that calm decisions do not result of necessity from states of any of the three classes of representations previously referred to, but are directly dependent upon the subject of willing itself, at least as decisions if not desires. However, all that is apprehended of the subject of willing is simply its willing, not some state preceding that willing, and from this we see that the law of causality — given that according to this every state is necessarily and always consequent upon a preceding state — does not apply to the will. On the other hand, because we necessarily presuppose that there is a sufficient reason for every decision, our own or someone else's, we are forced to hold that there is a specific form of the principle of sufficient reason governing here. I call this *the principle of sufficient reason of acting*, principium rationis sufficientis

54

agendi, or, more briefly, *the law of motivation*, employing the word *motive* to connote the reason presupposed.

§46 Motive, decision, empirical and intelligible characters

If we are required to give the motive for a decision, we refer to states of representations: either states of complete representations of the kind constituting the whole of experience, in which case the motive must be a relation among objects, or states of series of judgments that in the end are related to real objects — that is, have material truth, without which they could not provide a motive.[3]

A great deal of error occurs in the putting together of judgments, error of the sort that is avoided by wisdom; and, given that wisdom is so unevenly distributed, any state of real objects gives rise to judgments, and consequently to motives, of very different kinds. But even apart from this we are conscious of the inadequacy of explanations in terms of motives, since motives produce no more than desires: never decisions, the proper acts of will. Consequently, as far as decisions themselves are concerned, either we must view these as completely unconditioned and not subject to rule at all, or we must presuppose that for any given decision there is a state of the subject of willing constituting its necessary condition, a state that we are never able to apprehend because *the subject of willing* is only known *as willing* (that is, it is only known in individual acts of will), never in some state or other preceding it.[4] For while it is true that *desires* precede *decisions*, desires themselves are instances of willing, and nothing is explained by saying that of two conflicting desires the stronger becomes willing as a result of decision. What needs to be looked at is why the subject so strongly desires this or that: it is this that has to be seen either as occurring without rule or as resulting from a preceding state of the subject of willing. But this *state* cannot be apprehended, since it is not an object for the inner sense and therefore is *not a thing in time*. Even decisions are not things in time, and in this respect they resemble the present; for just as the present stands to the subject of knowing, so decisions appear to stand to the subject of willing. They constitute the point of contact between the subject of willing on the one hand, which lies outside of time and is unknowable, and motives on the other hand, which lie within time. We saw earlier that in the same fashion the present is the point of contact between, on the one hand, the subject of knowing which lies outside of time and is unknowable, and, on the other hand, objects which occupy time.

We assume that there is a perduring state of the subject of willing, and that decisions follow from it of necessity, because we notice that different individuals act in very different ways when prompted by similar observable motives, leaving aside any modifications due to different degrees of wisdom. By contrast, we notice that any individual in exactly the same circumstances acts in exactly the same way, acting therefore as it were in accordance with maxims. These maxims do not have to be present to the individual's reason in the form of abstract propositions, and he may have the liveliest conviction that he would be able to act in a totally different way if only he *wanted* to. That is, he may have the liveliest conviction that his will is not determined by anything outside it, and what is in question, therefore, is not *ability* to act, but whether there is such a thing as willing that is supremely free in its nature, independent of everything else and constituting man's inner essence.

The general manner of each person's acting, as *noticed* in the ways just mentioned, is his *empirical character*, and this can only be pieced together and inferred from his actions: it never presents itself as an immediate object of inner sense. However, although the expressions of a person's empirical character are each separate, they point to a unity and unalterability, and for this reason every empirical character must be thought of as the appearance of something utterly unknowable and existing outside of time, constituting as it were a permanent state of the subject of willing. I say 'as it were,' because *state* and *permanent* have application in time alone, and there is strictly speaking no way of expressing what is outside of time.

Perhaps I can better indicate what I mean, if only figuratively, by referring to what lies behind a person's empirical character as 'a timeless universal act of willing,' from which all acts occurring in time emerge as manifestations. Kant refers to this as the *intelligible character* (though it might more properly be called 'unintelligible'), and he provides us with a discussion of the differences between it and the *empirical* character, as well as of the whole relation between freedom and nature; a discussion that I consider to be an incomparable and wholly admirable masterpiece of profound human thought (*CPR*, pp. 560-586). Schelling likewise gives us a praiseworthy and illuminating account of it in the first volume of his *Writings* (pp. 465-473).

As throughout this treatise, my intention in making reference to these works is not to repeat what has been said elsewhere. I have limited myself to what I consider necessary and relevant to my present purposes, intending in general to exclude extraneous matter from this philosophical monograph, and specifically to exclude all treatment of ethics and aesthetics. These do not give rise to a new class of objects, and consequently, like so much else, do not require to be introduced in relation to my division of classes. Moreover, a consideration of them would fill a study on its own, a study that would be bound to exceed this treatise in scope and content and, however consonant with it, would read very differently.

If a man's empirical character were known perfectly, his behaviour would be predictable from the circumstances surrounding him and constituting the motives for his actions, and would follow from these according to rule as predictably as effects from known causes. None the less, there would always be need of an important *correction* to the predictions made, because of the difference between a man's circumstances, which are objective in belonging to the complete representation of an experience common to us all, and the judgments and series of judgments that he makes about them in accordance with the degree of sharpness of his understanding.

It is impossible to have complete knowledge of a man's empirical character or of the correction required for making predictions concerning his behaviour, since neither is given to us as an object. Rather, such knowledge as we have is pieced together from limited ranges of circumstances; and even of these it is impossible to have complete knowledge, since we can never know all the past and present impressions that have gone to modify a man's disposition as a result of his decisions, nor the judgments that have resulted from his reflections. Of course, some degree of knowledge is possible, and when this is attained it is often very real and of great use to people of the world. (Pragmatic psychology is the source of instruction in such knowledge when its aim is this usefulness to people of the world, while empirical psychology makes a more general study of it.)

The empirical character of animals is much easier to probe, since each species possesses a single character manifested in its individual members as clearly and with as little variation as the physical characteristics that typify it. It is because of this that the empirical character of a given species can easily be pieced together from experiments on individuals; anyone attentively observing cats, dogs or monkeys is very well able to predict how these will behave in specified circumstances. And in the case of lesser developed kinds the task is even easier, and the knowledge acquired has a higher degree of certainty; in the case of infusoria, their movements must even conform to mathematical patterns.

Where the human race is concerned, observation of the species as a whole provides what we call 'knowledge of men,' an unsystematic empirico-pragmatic psychology; but the principles of this psychology never furnish certainty, owing to the obvious existence of individual human characters, a phenomenon of freedom having its roots in reason and possessed by humans alone.

These reflections shed light on the difference between plays and novels on the one hand and the *Fables of Aesop* or *Reynard the Fox* on the other. In addition, they make clear why proper names in this last work coincide with the names of the species — Nodel the Lion, Isegrin the Wolf, Bruin the Bear; more properly speaking, they bring out why proper names here are pleonastic. Finally, they make clear why only humans have individual physiognomies, each animal species having but one, though of course the face of an individual animal, like its paws, can bear accidental differences.

Motives, then, are sufficient reasons for acting for the empirical character. But the circumstances constituting motives of actions are not the causes of those actions, producing them as effects, because actions arise not from circumstances but from the empirical character, which is not directly apprehensible: to repeat, it is inferred from and in some measure pieced together from the observation of actions. Actions arise from the empirical character under the promptings of motives.

The law of causality may be compared in one respect to the law of optics governing the way in which rays of light act on colourless and translucent bodies having parallel surfaces, or on colourless mirrors. Light traverses them or is reflected by them unaltered: a ray of light remains in the same state throughout its path, and from what it is like at the beginning we are able to predict what it will be like at the end. The law of motivation, by contrast, resembles the law of optics governing the way in which rays of light act on coloured bodies. Here, the same light is red when reflected from one body and green from another, while from a black body it is not reflected at all; and how bodies reflect light cannot be predicted from knowledge of their other characteristics, nor from knowledge of the other characteristics of light. It can only be predicted from observing what happens when the two come together.

On the other hand, any particular body reflects light in the same way on all occasions, because there is only one kind of light. If there were several, a selfsame body would be able to reflect yellow or red. And just as in that case it would be difficult to determine a body's colour, so now it is difficult to discern a person's empirical character. For this manifests itself under many kinds of influence, and the same person behaves in different ways under different influences, though always the same under the same influences. Even so, we see from the works of the great poets, especially those of Shakespeare, that it is possible to obtain such profound glimpses into the coloured ball of a man's empirical character that, given that these glimpses are beyond explanation, they point to a direct insight into his intelligible character.

In the first three forms of the principle of sufficient reason, described earlier, knowledge of a reason qua reason is always accompanied by knowledge of what is based upon that reason, and this warrants the making of a hypothetical judgment that has certainty. In the present form of the principle, by contrast, this is not so. For it is possible to know a person's motives without knowing how he will behave, given that every subject has its own empirical character which cannot be completely known.

The reason why the regularity governing the other forms of the principle of sufficient reason has no application here is that, while in their case we remain within the domain of lawfulness, here we enter a very different domain, that of freedom. Consequently, if I compare my descriptions of the first three forms of the principle of sufficient reason to moving images projected on to a wall from a magic lantern, in this case I must add an open hatch through which light enters and makes some of my images vanish while rendering the rest incoherent, confused and obscure.

§47 Causal influence of the will on knowing

The will is able to exert a causal influence not only on the immediate object and thereby on the external world, but on the knowing self as well: it can compel this to repeat earlier representations, to focus its attention in general on this or that, and to initiate any series of thoughts whatever. In particular, mental images as mentioned earlier are repetitions of representations previously present through the mediation of the immediate object. They themselves however are not produced in this mediate fashion, because of which they do not belong to the total complex of experience, unlike the immediate object, and do not come under the law of causality governing it. Instead they come under the law governing expressions of the will — the law of motivation — even in cases where we are not aware of the expressions in question but only of their immediate effects.

In cases where we are not aware of the will's expressions, things seem to come into our consciousness without being linked to anything else there. But that this is impossible is precisely the root of the principle of sufficient reason, as was mentioned earlier. Given the existence of this principle, an image appearing suddenly before our imagination, or even a judgment not following upon the reason immediately preceding it, must be the product of an act of will with a motive. The motive and the act of will in question often escape our notice, however, because the motive is insignificant and the act of will so effortless that it occurs simultaneously with the motive.

The motive giving rise to mental images, or even to judgments that are said to enter the mind suddenly, is normally the association of ideas: that is, the desire to have representations before us that are similar to those already present. And this act of will in turn is due to the motive constituted by our characteristic urge to perfect our knowledge (which accounts for its being stronger in intelligent people), an urge that we help to satisfy by bringing similar representations together and thereby fulfilling the law of homogeneity.

§48 Memory

The characteristic of the knowing subject in virtue of which it obeys the will in repeating representations with an ease proportionate to their past frequency — in other words, its *ability to function well as a result of practice*[5] — is what we call *memory*. The usual image for this is a storehouse for preserving a ready stock of completely determinate representations, whether we are conscious of these or not. I cannot accept such an image.

The repetition at will of past representations becomes so easy as a result of practice that, if one of a series comes before us, we at once call up the rest, often seemingly against our will; and if we want an image for this characteristic of our faculty of representations, I think the most apt is the image of a piece of cloth falling naturally into settled pleats if frequently folded in the same way. (Plato's simile is that of a soft mass retaining imprints.) Just as the body through practice learns to obey the will, so it is with the faculty of representations. By contrast, what an individual instance of remembering is certainly not is what common description takes it to be, namely a representation as it were brought out of storage. The truth of the matter rather is that every representation is genuinely new, even if thanks to practice it arises with peculiar ease. It is owing to this that our mental images, which we think of as stored away in memory (though really our memory is simply being repeatedly exercised), undergo changes unnoticed, a fact that we are made aware of when after a long interval we come across something that in the past we have been familiar with and discover that it does not fully match our picture of it. This could not occur if we stored fully detailed representations within us — a point made by Plato, or something like it, in the *Symposium* (pp. 240f.).

All of this explains why the surroundings and events of childhood are so deeply impressed upon our memories. As children we have few representations and almost all of them are complete, and we endlessly repeat these for the sake of occupying our minds. Moreover, what is true of children in this respect is true throughout their lives of men endowed with little ability to think for themselves: true, moreover, in respect of objects of reason as well as complete representations. Because of this, indeed, unless they are abnormally dull and obtuse, such men often have excellent memories. By contrast, men of genius often lack good memories, because their constant streams of new thoughts and trains of thought leave them little time for repetition; on the other hand, they are not often found to have particularly bad memories, since their greater energy and quickness of mind makes up for their want of practice.

It has been remarked that men who are always reading novels lose their power of memory, and the explanation of this is that the number of their representations leaves them little time or patience for repetition and practice. In this they are like men of genius, though in their case it is not their own ideas and trains of thought that pass rapidly before their minds, but the compositions of others; in addition, they lack the force of mind possessed by men of genius to compensate for want of practice.

It is not difficult to see that representations connected by the thread of one or more of the kinds of reason and consequent considered in this treatise are more easily retained than those connected solely with the will and produced by it in accordance with the law of motivation: in other words, put together by choice. In representations of the former kind, thanks to our a priori knowledge of their formal elements, we are relieved of half the effort usually required, and it was probably this, together with a priori knowledge in general, that prompted Plato's doctrine that learning is but remembering.

§49 Feelings and the like

Feelings, emotions, passions and the like, given that we are aware of them, are plainly objects for the subject, and as such must either fall within the classes of objects considered in this treatise, or make up a class of their own. My conclusion is that they are all reducible to one or other of the following.

1) Bodily feelings. The extremes of these are pain and sensual delight, and between the two there are endless modifications. They are states of the immediate object, and as such fall under the law of causality.

However, the subject of willing, in virtue of its causal influence upon the subject of knowing, can get the subject of knowledge to focus upon objects other than the immediate object and its states.

2) Acts of the will. Among these I number longing, fear, hatred, anger, grief, joy and the like, each constituting an instance of an ardent want for something to happen or not to happen in cases where the causal efficacy of the want is frustrated by some other want or by external obstacles. It is this very frustration that raises the level of the want to a high pitch of intensity, rather as resistance raises the strength of electricity.

Joy is a want suddenly released from its frustrations and consequently satisfied. Sorrow is a continuing want for something recognised to be impossible of attainment, in the face of which the sensible person will say, 'I have good reason to be dejected, but will not be.'

As acts of will, all of the above come under the law of motivation. The body, the immediate object of willing as well as of knowing, is almost always affected by them, and bodily feelings accompany them and merge with them. But that these feelings are acts of will is clear from the universal demand made upon us that we control and indeed suppress them: in other words, that we so raise their opposing desires to the status of willing that through continual suppression they no longer arise. But when the opposite to this occurs, and desires so violent determine a man's empirical character that their opposites seem no longer capable of arising, and the man as if through suspension of his use of reason becomes virtually indistinguishable from an animal, we call such desires *passions*.

3) Composites of bodily states and acts of will. An indistinctly recognised but unpleasant affection of the body gives rise to a resolve to be rid of it; but given that the object of this resolve is correspondingly ill discerned, the mind seeks other objects for it. This is hypochondria. A sudden cessation of a bodily affection of this sort, together with release from the frustrated resolve which is without a clear object, is called a *feeling of well being*. And so on.

People also speak of moral, religious and aesthetic feelings, but I strongly disapprove of these expressions, and cannot accept them as valid. This is not because I wish to preserve my own scheme of classification intact, but for another and perfectly sound reason, namely that such expressions have their origin in a form of blind *syncretism*.[6] This error, concerning itself with utterly inessential characteristics, includes under a single category all that is best in man on the one hand — indeed that in comparison with which the rest of reality stands as the shadow of a dream to a real and solid body — and a variety of quite different things on the other hand, among which is what is purely animal or worse in human nature. It includes all of these under a single category and indiscriminately calls them *feelings*.

Because of my already mentioned resolve to avoid ethics and aesthetics in this treatise, I cannot go further into this topic here. For, as in the anatomical preparation of a single bodily part, so in writing a monograph: one must pay attention to those places where it has been severed from other parts of the whole that it essentially belongs to, and where the natural unity of the whole has been violently and quite arbitrarily destroyed.

Notes

1 Re intellecta, in verbis simus faciles.
2 Wollen κατ' ἐξοχήν.
3 Consideration of the morality of actions alters nothing here. For the moral maxims that actions come under do not constitute motives but general expressions for certain classes of motives. When Arnold von Winkelried embraces the enemy spears, the motive of his action is his country's distress that he seeks to avert. The maxim according to which we should not prefer our own well being to that of others, to the general well being, a maxim that does not need to be known to the agent *in abstracto*, is merely the expression of what is common to many motives, in respect of which a subject is said to be *good* who allows himself to be determined by motives of this nature. A person who does not return what is entrusted to his keeping has as his motive a conviction that wealth furthers his own well being. The maxim according to which one should in every way further one's own well being is merely an expression for what is common to many motives. The subject whose actions follow from motives of this character is said to be *bad*. The maxim need not for this purpose be known *in abstracto*.
4 This same qualification is to be understood where the subject of willing is portrayed above as the object of inner sense.

5   Its *Uebungsfähigkeit* (FW).
6   What I understand by this here is the opposite of *criticism*, in the original sense of that word — that is, differentiation carried out in full. Syncretism therefore is the confounding of what is different.

8 General remarks and conclusions

§50 Transition

The preceding four chapters contain a detailed presentation of the four applications of the principle of sufficient reason and the corresponding laws of our faculty of knowledge from which they stem — laws that appear to be interrelated and to constitute modifications of but a single law.

Nothing remains to be done but add some reflections on the principle of sufficient reason in general and on its four forms.

§51 Other principles of the fourfold division of reasons

I distinguished and divided the forms of the principle of sufficient reason in accordance with the classes of possible objects for our faculty of representation, and in doing so set myself the task of two investigations instead of one.

It is easy to see that I could more simply have followed Kant's basic principles and appealed to the four faculties of the mind to make my division, arguing as follows: the principle of reason of becoming, as the law of causality, lies in our *understanding*; the principle of reason of knowing lies in our *reason*, this being the faculty of inference; the principle of reason of being lies in our *pure sensibility*; the law of motivation governs the *will*. Alternatively, I could have made my division in accordance with the divisions introduced by Kant, allotting the principle of causality to *transcendental logic*, the principle governing reasons of knowing to *general logic*, the principle governing reasons of being to *transcendental aesthetic*, and the law of motivation to *ethics*.

However, the division that I favour has its justification. This in part lies in the method of accounting for it, a method that both introduces incidental topics at least as interesting as the principal topic of inquiry, and enables the principal inquiry itself to be given a thorough treatment that would otherwise not have been accorded it; in part it lies in the fact that in the course of the investigation the following significant result is brought more clearly to light: the four laws of knowledge do not merely find common expression in the principle of sufficient reason, but at an altogether fundamental level constitute a single law assuming different forms according to the diversity of *objects* existing for our faculty of knowledge.

§52 The systematic order

The order in which I have stated the different applications of the principle of sufficient reason is not the systematic order, but one chosen purely for the sake of clarity, beginning with what is better known and least presupposes the rest. Even so, this purpose of mine will not have been entirely achieved, and, because of the interrelatedness of the parts of my treatise, anyone wishing to understand it completely will need to read it twice.

The systematic order in which the kinds of reason should be stated is this. First, the principle of reason of being applied to *time*, on the grounds that this is the simple schema containing only what is essential in the other forms of the principle; indeed it constitutes the very prototype of the finite. Second, the principle of reason of being in space. Third, the law of causality. Fourth, the law of motivation. Fifth, the principle of sufficient reason of knowing, stated last because, unlike the others which are concerned with representations, it is concerned with representations of representations.

§53 Relation of time between reason and consequent

Where the laws of causality and motivation apply, reasons necessarily precede their consequents in time; and if we reflect that it is not things that cause things, but states that cause states, we shall not be misled on this point by examples of the sort given by Kant, who asserts that the heat of a room and the stove causing it are simultaneous (*CPR*, p. 248). This is not so. The state of the stove, having a temperature higher than that of the surrounding medium, necessarily precedes the passing on of its surplus heat to that medium; and because each layer of air on becoming hot gives way to a colder layer flowing in, the first state, which is the cause, and consequently the second state also, which is the effect, are renewed continuously, as long as stove and room differ in temperature. It follows that there is not a perduring cause, a stove, and a perduring effect simultaneous with it, heat, but an endlessly renewed sequence of two states, one the effect of the other.

The same is true of the law of motivation. The motive always comes before the decision, and the decision itself, given that it is a pure point in time (the point of contact between subject and object), is even without duration. By contrast, the principle of sufficient reason of knowing does not entail a temporal relation, but only a relation for our faculty of reason. Consequently, *before* and *after* are meaningless here.

64

In the same way, the principle of sufficient reason of being as applied to geometry does not involve a temporal relation but one that is purely spatial, and everything in space could be said to be simultaneous were it not for the fact that the notion of simultaneity, like that of succession, has no meaning here. In arithmetic, on the other hand, the reason of being is neither more nor less than temporal relatedness itself.

§54 Reciprocity of reasons

Each application of the principle of sufficient reason can support hypothetical judgments (though, as was said earlier, judgments based on the law of motivation never afford certainty), and the laws of hypothetical inferences remain valid here.

These laws are the following. From the existence of a reason it is valid to infer the existence of its corresponding consequent, and from the nonexistence of a consequent the non-existence of its reason. From the nonexistence of a reason it is invalid to infer the non-existence of its consequent, or from the existence of a consequent the existence of its reason. In geometry, however, it is strangely possible in virtually all cases to infer from the existence of a consequent the existence of its reason, and from the non-existence of a reason the non-existence of its consequent. This is because each line determines the position of all others, as was shown in Section 38, and consequently it is a matter of indifference where a start is made. In other words, it is a matter of indifference which line is treated as reason and which as consequent.

It is possible to convince oneself of this by working through the theorems of geometry. It is only in cases where areas are considered independently of figures rather than figures themselves — in other words, rather than linear positions — that it is usually impossible to infer from the existence of a consequent the existence of its reason, or rather to change the propositions about and make the conditioned the condition. The following will serve as an example of this. The proposition, 'If triangles have equal bases and heights, they have equal areas,' cannot be converted to the proposition, 'If triangles have equal areas, they have equal bases and heights,' since, where triangles are equal in area, their bases and heights are interchangeable.

§55 Series of reasons and consequents

According to the law of causality, whatever is a condition is itself conditioned, conditioned moreover in the same manner. As a consequence, there is an infinite series of causes preceding any given cause.[1] The same is true of reasons of being in space: every relative space constitutes a figure and possesses boundaries linking it to a further relative space, in turn determining the figure of this latter, and so on indefinitely along all dimensions.[2] On the other hand, if we take a particular figure by itself, the series of reasons of being has a terminus, because we start from a given relation; just as a series of causes has a terminus if we stop at a particular cause. By contrast, what constitutes the series of reasons of being in time has an unending duration in respect of the past but only of the past,[3] since every given moment is conditioned by an earlier one but not a later one, even though it unfailingly points towards a later one. On the other hand, a series of reasons of knowing, in other words a series of judgments each of which endows its successor with logical truth, always comes to an end in a truth that is empirical, metaphysical or metalogical.

In the first of these cases, where a series of reasons ends in an empirical truth, if we go on asking 'Why?' what we are asking for is a cause. In other words, the series of reasons of knowing becomes a series of reasons of becoming. In the other two cases, where a series of reasons ends in a truth that is either metaphysical or metalogical, there is no way of answering 'Why?' since the question itself makes no sense, and there is no knowing what kind of reason is being sought.

Motives also form into series, since a decision in favour of an end becomes a motive for deciding on a series of means to achieve that end. But in respect of its antecedent part,[4] any such series ends in a representation from one of the first two classes, and the fact that a definite representation from either of these becomes a motive contributes to our knowledge of the empirical character of the subject. On the other hand, there is no saying why this or that representation becomes a motive, since the intelligible character of the subject lies outside of time, and can therefore never constitute an object. It follows that any series of motives comes to an end in a representation of one or other of the first two classes.

§56 Confirmation from languages

It may be that languages contain particular expressions for the four different kinds of reason, though this is a supposition needing confirmation from linguistic research. I think, for example, that in cases where consequents are derived directly from their reasons, different sets of words indicate the different kinds of consequence, though exact observation of this usage is unlikely to be found everywhere in literature, since it requires both sensitivity and close attention. To give instances of what I mean, I think that the words *ergo, folglich* and *sintemal* express consequence from a reason of knowing or a reason of being; *inde, quare* and *daher* consequence from a reason of becoming; *igitur, quamobrem* and *also* consequence from a reason of acting.

§57 Every science has one form of the principle of reason rather than others as its main thread

Since the question 'Why?' is always a demand for a sufficient reason, and since it is the close tie among instances of knowledge in accordance with the principle of sufficient reason that distinguishes a science from a mere aggregate of such instances, it was said in Section 4 that *why* is the mother of the sciences. It is further true that in each of the sciences one particular form of the principle of sufficient reason is the main thread running through it, even though other forms have application there of a secondary kind. The principle of reason of being is the main thread in pure mathematics (though the exposition of proofs is merely in accordance with reasons of knowing). In applied mathematics the law of causality is equally a main thread, and this same law assumes supremacy in physics, chemistry, geology, and so on. The principle of reason of knowing is prominent in all of the sciences, since in all of them knowledge of the particular is obtained from the general, but it constitutes the main and almost exclusive thread in botany, zoology, mineralogy and the rest of the classificatory sciences. The law of motivation is the main thread in history, politics, practical psychology, and so on, where all motives and maxims, irrespective of their kind, are considered as the data from which to explain behaviour; but where motives and maxims as such, their value and origin, are under consideration, the law of motivation is the main thread of ethics.

§58 A vindication regarding imagination and reason

I think that I need to take up two points before concluding my treatise. I made some comments in Section 22 concerning the imagination that will displease those judging this to be man's noblest possession and the well-spring of poets and artists. Further on, in Sections 27 and 33, I outlined and gave a description of reason that is correspondingly unlikely to satisfy those who judge *this* to be man's most valuable possession, basing their judgment on the conviction that it is reason — where 'reason' is accompanied by the predicate 'practical' — that engenders virtue and saintliness. It is even less likely to satisfy those who speak of reason as a 'faculty of absolute knowledge,' according it an apotheosis quite out of keeping with what I have said of it. Both of these views concerning the imagination and reason are widespread, and both are held by worthy and thoughtful persons. Consequently, in the hope of effecting some sort of reconciliation, I offer the following comments. Imagination is not the essential and inner force that produces poets or artists, but it is none the less a necessary condition of becoming a poet or an artist, even if it is a condition that is as it were merely adventitious and extraneous. Indeed it is just as much a condition of gross stupidity as of poetic or artistic genius, which shows that in itself it is merely a tool and whatever else I described it as in Section 22.

To come now to reason. According to my description of it, but contrary to the teaching of Kant, of his successors, and of almost all philosophers since Descartes, reason is not the source of virtue and saintliness. Rather, it is simply the faculty of concepts and behaviour in accordance with these, and as such it is no more than a necessary condition of virtue and saintliness. Consequently, it too is no more than a tool, and in fact is just as much a necessary condition of villainy as of virtue and saintliness, of being the sort of person that Plato refers to as a tyrant and describes so brilliantly in the eighth and ninth books of the *Republic*.

What then is the innermost nature of the artist and the saint, if indeed they share the same nature? To go into this here would be contrary to my resolve not to consider ethics and aesthetics in this treatise, but the question could at some time furnish me with the topic of a larger work and a work of a kind that would stand to the present treatise as waking stands to dreaming. And to counter any misconstrual of this expression as critical of my investigation, now drawing to a close, I appeal to the words of Seneca: *Somnia narrare vigilantis est.*[5]

§59 Two principal results

In this treatise I have been at pains to show that the principle of sufficient reason is a general expression for four very different relations, each resting on a different law given to us a priori (the principle of sufficient reason being a synthetic a priori truth). The basic principle of *homogeneity* obliges us to assume that these laws, discovered in accordance with the basic principle of *specification*, have as their common root a single fundamental characteristic of our whole faculty of knowledge, just as correspondingly they are united in having a common expression.

This common root therefore may be seen as the innermost seed of all the dependency, relativity, instability and finite character of the objects of our consciousness, itself confined to sensibility, understanding, reason, subject and object. In other words, it may be seen as the innermost seed of this world that the sublime Plato repeatedly disparages, referring to it as that which is for ever coming into being and perishing and never really existing at all,⁶ stating further that knowledge of it is nothing but belief based upon perception without the ability to give an account of itself.⁷ This is the world that Christendom — with unerring instinct and in keeping with that form of the principle of sufficient reason referred to in Section 52 as its simplest schema and the prototype of all that is finite — refers to as *temporality*.

If I have succeeded in establishing this result in my treatise, I think that any philosopher who rests a conclusion on the principle of sufficient reason in the course of his speculations, or speaks of a 'reason' at all, should be required to specify which form of the principle and which kind of reason he has in mind. It might be thought that this would occur as a matter of course whenever a reason is in question, and that consequently no confusion would be possible. But this is not so. There are far too many cases where the expressions 'reason' and 'cause' are confused or employed interchangeably, and too many where there is *general* talk of reason and what is based upon reason, or of principle and what is derived from principle, or again of condition and conditioned, without any further qualification — perhaps because those employing such concepts are secretly aware of using them for transcendent purposes.

Even Kant is guilty here. He speaks of his notorious *thing in itself* as the *reason* of phenomenal reality. He speaks of a *reason of the possibility* of all phenomena, of an *intelligible reason* of phenomena, of an *intelligible cause* of phenomena, and of an *unknown reason* of the possibility of sensuous series in general (*CPR*, pp. 590, 592). He speaks of a *transcendental object* as constituting the *reason* of phenomena, of the *reason* why our sensibility has the principal conditions that it has rather than others (p. 641). And so on in similar vein elsewhere. These expressions are utterly out of keeping with those weighty, profound, and indeed immortal words of his: 'The contingency of things is *itself merely phenomenal*, and the only kind of regressus it can lead to is empirical, a regressus determining phenomena (p. 591).'⁸ Anyone familiar with recent philosophical writings will know that the concepts of *reason* and *consequent, principle* and *what is derived from principle*, and so on, have been used since the time of Kant in an even less precise sense, and employed for transcendent purposes. However, I prefer to take my examples from Kant's own writings, even though they are less graphic than some that might be taken from elsewhere, because it is not my intention to be critical but to make my views clear by examples.

My objection to these imprecise ways of using the word *reason*, and to correspondingly imprecise ways of employing the principle of sufficient reason, constitutes the second but closely related result of this treatise concerning its own subject-matter. The objection goes as follows. The four laws of our faculty of knowledge, whose common expression is the principle of sufficient reason, have their source in a single, fundamental characteristic and inner nature of our consciousness, manifested in the forms of sensibility, understanding and reason. This is easy to discern and is obvious from the common character of the laws themselves, and from the fact that all objects for subjects are divided exhaustively among them, in such wise that if we were to imagine a fifth class of objects, we should have to assume a fifth form of the principle of sufficient reason governing it. But none of this justifies our speaking of a *reason pure and simple*. There no more exists a *reason in general* than a *triangle in general*, except as a purely abstract concept — that is, except as a representation of representations derived in discursive reasoning and constituting nothing more than a means of thinking many things in one. Every triangle must be acute-angled, right-angled or obtuse-angled, equilateral, isosceles or scalene. Similarly, every reason must belong to one of the four possible kinds that I have stated, and therefore be valid within and only within one of the four well distinguished classes of objects for our faculty of representation — the only four that there are. Consequently, its use presupposes these classes together with our faculty of representation — in other words, the whole world — and confines itself within them.

If anyone thinks otherwise, believing that reason in general is more than a concept drawn from the four kinds of reason and expressing what they have in common, we may find ourselves reviving the controversy between realists and nominalists, and in this context I should have to be on the side of the nominalists.

Notes

1 Und so entsteht a parte priori eine series in indefinitum.
2 Nach allen Dimensionen in indefinitum.
3 A parte priori.
4 A parte priori.
5 As employed by Seneca himself (*Ep.* 53, 8, 2, though Seneca employs the word *somnium*, not *somnia*), this expression means that only a waking person can narrate dreams — that to narrate one's dreams is proof that one is awake. But the Latin can bear other meanings — that it is the duty of waking persons to narrate their dreams, that it characteristic of, or usual for, waking persons to narrate their dreams, and so on. (FW).
6 ἀεὶ γιγνόμενον μὲν καὶ ἀπολλύμενον, ὄντως δὲ οὐδέποτε ὄν.
7 δόξα μετ' αἰσθήσεως ἀλόγου.
8 What is in question here is empirical contingency, which is tantamount to dependency on other things. The note on the thesis of the

69

fourth antimony provides convincing evidence of this. (A *regressus* in logic is a form of argument proceeding 'back' from particular to general, conditioned to condition, effect to cause (FW).)

9 General survey with comments on Schopenhauer's text, by F.C. White

Schopenhauer's three introductory chapters

Chapter one. The main task that Schopenhauer sets himself in the *Fourfold Root* is an examination of the principle of sufficient reason, the principle that he considers to be the foundation of all systematic knowledge. Accordingly, he opens his first chapter by outlining the method that he proposes to employ in undertaking this examination. He will apply what he calls the laws of 'homogeneity' and 'specification,' laws that he claims are recommended to us by Plato and Kant, the philosophers that he reveres before all others. These laws, he asserts twice in his first section, are transcendental and a priori, thereby ensuring that everything conforms to them, and given the importance of the doctrine behind this terminology, and its wide application throughout the *Fourfold Root*, it will be useful to say something about it straight away.

Many of Schopenhauer's central arguments, like many of Kant's, begin by assuming that there are true propositions known to us a priori which are both necessary and universal in their application. 'Two straight lines cannot enclose a space' will serve as an example. Schopenhauer believes that this proposition is known to us a priori—that is, known to us 'before' experience in the sense of not relying for its justification upon the evidence of experience. He further believes that it is necessarily true and universal in its application: in other words, he believes that it is not possible for any two straight lines to enclose a space. Most importantly, and again with Kant, he believes that the explanation of this is not that the proposition, 'Two straight lines cannot enclose a space,' is true of reality as reality necessarily and universally is in itself and independently of us, but that its truth is a projection of our minds, reflecting their essential and unalterable structures. This is what he means by saying that such propositions are 'transcendental.'

With this in mind we can now turn to the substance of the supposedly transcendental laws of homogeneity and specification. The first of these requires us to take note of similarities among things, and consequently to group them under kinds. The second by contrast requires us to take note of dissimilarities and so to avoid blurring important distinctions. As it turns out, Schopenhauer's real concern in the *Fourfold Root* is to apply the second law to the principle of sufficient reason, establishing what he believes to be the irreducibly different forms of that principle and the correspondingly different kinds of necessity that these impose upon our view of phenomenal reality. He hopes that such a task, which he believes not to have been attempted before, will bring increased clarity to philosophy, at the same time ridding it of errors that result from confusing one form of the principle with another.

Why does Schopenhauer think that the principle of sufficient reason is worthy of scrutiny? Because he believes that it converts this or that set of otherwise disparate and disjointed pieces of knowledge into a science. Indeed a science is correctly described, he believes, as a set of systematically interrelated truths, each constituting a sufficient reason for another. Of every true proposition we can ask why it is true, he asserts, and in principle obtain an answer constituting a sufficient reason for its being so.

Schopenhauer concludes his first chapter by noting that while the purpose of his treatise is to distinguish the different forms of the principle of sufficient reason, he needs a general formulation of it to start with, and the formulation that he proposes as most useful is that of Christian Wolff: *Nothing is without a reason why it is rather than not.*

Chapter two. Schopenhauer now briefly considers the views of earlier philosophers on the principle of sufficient reason. Plato and Aristotle, he affirms, showed some awareness of the principle and considered it to be self-evident, and Aristotle, albeit unsatisfactorily, even distinguished various kinds of cause and various kinds of reason. Schopenhauer does not pause to discuss why he considers Aristotle's divisions to be unsatisfactory, but proceeds immediately to the assertion that Leibniz was the first to state the principle formally and in general terms, and the first clearly to distinguish two of its kinds, namely the principle that every change in the external world must have a cause constituting a sufficient reason for its occurrence, and the principle that every true judgment must have a rational ground or sufficient reason for its truth.

Schopenhauer backtracks a little here and turns to Descartes and Spinoza, accusing them — with little argument — of confusing the notions of *cause* and *rational ground*. Descartes talks of the immensity of God's nature as the *cause or reason* for His not needing a cause in order to exist, and from this it is plain, believes Schopenhauer, that he has no grasp of the radical difference between causes and rational grounds.[1]

Schopenhauer now briefly considers the successors of Leibniz. Wolff, he says, accepts the distinction drawn by Leibniz between causes and reasons, but then falls into confusion himself, and the philosophers between Wolff and Kant add nothing worth while to the discussion; in fact they too fall into confusion. Even Kant does nothing to advance our understanding of the principle of sufficient reason, since while he recognises the distinction between causes and rational grounds, he none the less goes on to say things that give rise to obscurities and misconceptions. Finally, while many writers after Kant are clear about the distinction, they add nothing of significance to the inquiry.

After this brief historical survey, traversing the terrain of western philosophy within the compass of some seven pages, Schopenhauer turns to arguing that the principle of sufficient reason cannot be proved. His argument is discouragingly brief, and to make sense of it requires guesswork and some borrowing from what is said later on; but in outline it seems to be something like this. The principle of sufficient reason, though capable of receiving a general formulation, is not really one principle at all. It is four. We are not told at this stage what the four are, but for the sake of convenience it will be useful to have them stated here. They are as follows: every change has a cause as its sufficient reason; the truth of every judgment is supported by a rational ground; the existence of every set of mathematical properties is grounded in some other set of mathematical properties; every action has a motive.

When we consider these principles in turn, thinks Schopenhauer, we see that each of them constitutes an irreducible condition of thought and knowledge, or — to use a more recent expression — we see that each of them constitutes an ultimate presupposition. But no non-circular proof is possible of ultimate presuppositions, since their being ultimate entails that no further propositions can serve as premises from which to prove them. (Kant's transcendental 'deduction' therefore demonstrates at best that the principle of causality and other such principles are ultimate presuppositions; it does not and could not prove them.)

If Schopenhauer's argument is in fact as I have presented it, it is a good argument, but only if it is plausible to assert that there are such things as ultimate presuppositions in the first place, and only if it is plausible further to assert that the different forms of the principle of sufficient reason are themselves ultimate presuppositions.[2] It must be conceded that neither assertion is obvious, and it is doubtful that all of Schopenhauer's forms of the principle of sufficient reason, at any rate as he states them, are even true. Certainly many philosophers reject the assertion that every change has a cause or that every action has a motive. These are points that will be returned to.

Chapter three. In this chapter Schopenhauer argues that the two applications of the principle of sufficient reason mentioned so far, that a change must have a cause and that a true judgment must have a rational ground, are not the only ones, and by means of the following examples he introduces two further applications. If a triangle has equal sides, this is *because* it has equal angles, but the 'because' here does not imply that the equality of the angles is the *cause* of the equality of the sides. For no *change* is in question, and Schopenhauer believes not implausibly that only changes can be causes. Nor does the 'because' imply that the equality of the angles is the *rational ground* of the equality of the sides, since a rational ground is a relation between concepts or judgments, and the relation between angles and sides is not of that kind. Of what kind then is it? It is a relation of *being*. To put Schopenhauer's point rather differently, the relation is not causal, nor is it a relation between the concepts of sides and angles, nor again between judgments about these: it is a relation between the angles and sides themselves. The sides *are* equal because the angles *are* equal. Moreover, the relation is a necessary one: the sides *must* be equal given the equality of the angles. This may sound Platonic, but in Schopenhauer's mind it is nothing of the sort. His view is the Kantian one that our minds intuit space and its properties, and consequently intuit the properties of individual lines, figures, areas, and so on. They also intuit the relations that these bear to one another. However, space and its properties are merely projections of our minds, so that triangles are not Platonic Forms, 'mathematicals,' or anything else of a realist sort, but aspects of the Kantian form of space, the form of our faculty of outer sensibility.

Schopenhauer's second example is as follows. If I ask why you are performing this or that action, you will reply by telling me your motive. What then is the relation between your action and your motive? It is not a relation between a judgment and its ground, since this time a change *is* at stake, not a judgment. Is the relation causal, then, is your motive the *cause* of your action? No. For while effects of their nature necessarily follow upon their causes, actions do not follow of necessity upon their motives: it is never possible to say that given such and such a motive this or that action will follow of necessity. In short, effects are determined by their causes, actions are not determined by their motives. Actions and motives, therefore, cannot stand in the relation of effects to causes.

Schopenhauer now moves on to two further important questions, the first of which is, 'What do all cases of the principle of sufficient reason have in common?' In other words, what does the principle of sufficient reason express *in general*? His answer is central to his system of thought as a whole and goes in summary as follows. Our consciousness comprises nothing but subject and objects — or, what comes to the same thing, subject and representations. But no representation existing in isolation can be an object for a subject. On the contrary, all representations are necessarily interconnected, all are governed by rules determinable a priori. It is precisely this necessary interconnectedness of representations that constitutes the metaphysical underpinning of the principle of sufficient reason. In other words, the principle of sufficient reason understood generally expresses the underlying fact that representations are necessarily interconnected. Indeed it is this interconnectedness that constitutes the root of the principle of sufficient reason.

Given its central role in Schopenhauer's thesis, this is worth expanding a little. According to Schopenhauer, our consciousness at bottom is made up of subject and object inseparably, or subject and objects inseparably — objects being such things as tables, chairs and concepts.[3] Further, these objects exist only because our mental faculties project their structures or forms on to what is presented to them: that is, they project time, space and such Kantian categories as causality, existence and substance on to original data. Finally, the most important feature of the resulting world of objects or representations is that these are interrelated and give rise to the principle of sufficient reason in its several forms. As a result of this, there are necessarily answers to questions of the following kinds: 'Why did that chair fall?' 'Why is the proposition true that the earth is a planet? 'Why do the angles of a triangle add up to 180°?' 'Why did Caesar cross the Rubicon?' Further, it is this interlocking of representations that makes science possible.

This in general terms is what Schopenhauer holds concerning the principle of sufficient reason — that its root is constituted by the underlying and necessary interconnectedness of representations — and he now applies the law of specification formally to it, asserting that it comprises four kinds and, perhaps more importantly, that each of these kinds is dependent for its nature upon one of the four classes that representations belong to. In later chapters, these classes will be treated separately, as will be their related forms of the principle of sufficient reason.

Schopenhauer adds that there is no way of arguing deductively for his division of representations into four classes. Like Kant's list of categories, he says, his division rests upon induction, and the most that may be done by way of defending it is to challenge dissenters to come forward with additional classes or to show that the classes he proposes are reducible to fewer.

It is a pity that Schopenhauer does not stop to defend his fourfold division, since many philosophers have a different way of seeing the world. To illustrate the point, some hold that the irreducible components of phenomenal reality are sense-data, universals, and minds; others that reality contains nothing but material substances; others again that it contains nothing but spacetime and modifications of spacetime. Schopenhauer himself was aware of the competing classifications of such philosophers as Plato, Aristotle and Descartes, but he assumes without argument that they are wrong.

Similarly, when it comes to his principles of explanation, it is a pity again that Schopenhauer does not stop to argue for his divisions. He accuses Descartes, Spinoza and even Kant of confusing the notions of reason and cause, but it is not implausible to hold that he is guilty of a kindred confusion himself in what concerns human action. The only real explanation of an action, it might sensibly be asserted, consists in giving the agent's *reasons* for doing it, and that consequently motives are not causes, as Schopenhauer in the end effectively believes,[4] but reasons.

The remark must be added, however, that whatever weaknesses attach to Schopenhauer's individual conclusions, his general venture is beyond reproach. It is undoubtedly one of the main tasks of metaphysics, perhaps the only one, to establish what objects are comprised in reality and what principles govern them.

The first class of objects and the first form of the principle of sufficient reason: chapter four

The objects that constitute the first class are for the most part complete representations, together forming 'a totality of experience.' To put this in more common terms, they are physical or material objects, so interrelated that they make up a single public world of human experience — the world of mountains and trees, of tables and chairs. To say that they are complete means that they possess not only formal properties like being spatial, temporal and causally interconnected, but material properties like being red, smooth and heavy. To say that they form a totality of experience means that they constitute a single world: they coexist, are subject to changes of state in a common space and time, are causally interrelated, and so on. Schopenhauer explains this, in keeping with the Kantian tradition, by saying that the forms of the faculties of inner and outer sensibility are united by the faculty of understanding through the imposition of its categories,[5] and that as a result of this the objective, real world is created.

The real world

Schopenhauer now discusses what he means by the *real* world, and points out what he considers to be a number of errors concerning its nature, together with one important source of these errors. All representations, he says, are presented to us *immediately* in time alone. To put his point rather differently: as far as immediate consciousness goes, we are presented with nothing but a flux of immediate representations, which are converted into the public world of common experience only through the work of the understanding in uniting space and time through the imposition of its categories.

Schopenhauer believes that many philosophers — best described here perhaps as 'independent realists' — fail to grasp this. They falsely assume that representations as immediately presented to us in time alone are indeed representations — that is, objects existing only for subjects and inseparably from these — but that as forming part of the totality of experience they are real in the sense of existing absolutely, independently of all subjects. This is a serious error. All representations, whether considered as immediately present or as parts of the totality of experience, are objects, and as such are inseparable from subjects. There are no such things as objects without subjects, no such things as subjects without objects.

It is not clear which philosophers Schopenhauer is thinking of here who assume both that representations are present to us in time alone and that they constitute parts of the totality of experience, but we can best understand his objection if we think of them as causal realists. According to such philosophers, while purely subjective states are all that we are immediately aware of, these are caused by physical objects existing independently of us, capable therefore of existing as objects without subjects. Schopenhauer's objection to this doctrine is, perhaps justifiably, that we have no grounds for talking of such things as objects without subjects, since whatever we think of is in some sense known to us, and therefore presupposes us as subjects. At the same time, there are no such things as states of awareness that are in every sense subjective, since to be aware is *eo ipso* to be aware of an object or objects.

Schopenhauer now goes on to make a point which is not altogether clear but seems to be something like this. The distinction between subject and object, knower and known, is the most fundamental fact about reality ever adverted to, and is reflected in such languages as employ different words for the being of subjects and the being of objects. To take examples, English says 'I *am*,' but 'he, she or it *is*;' Latin says 'ego *sum*,' but 'ille, illa, illud *est*;' German says 'ich *bin*,' but 'er, sie, es *ist*.' At the same time, however, each of these languages employs a general word to connote being: English employs 'being' or 'to be;' Latin employs 'esse;' German employs 'sein.' Unfortunately, this fact has led philosophers in the past to blur the distinction between subject and object, and to talk about the *being* or *reality* of, say, subjects, as though these could have absolute reality, existing independently of objects. However, as long as we keep to such expressions as 'I *am*' and 'he, she, it *is*,' we shall not fall into this error concerning the ontological status of subjects — imagining them to be separable from objects. By contrast, if we start talking about subjects as *being* or as having *existence*, we shall run the risk of thinking of them as existing in their own right, independently of objects. We shall run the risk of thinking of subjects as Cartesian selves or souls.[6]

Schopenhauer's comments here on the influence of language have a curiously twentieth-century ring; indeed it has been frequently argued in this century, however implausibly, that language is the prime source of metaphysical muddles.

The body

An interesting question now to be answered is this. How do immediate representations in time come to be present to us? What, so to speak, is the mechanism here? Schopenhauer's answer is that immediate representations are *effects*, causally produced in us through the instrumentality of the body, which latter he refers to as the 'immediate object.' This does not mean, however, that I apprehend nothing more than effects in my mind: rather, owing to the part played by my understanding, I apprehend the causes of these effects as substrata and substances existing in space. In other words, Schopenhauer's view is something like this. Suppose that I perceive a table, as we say. What happens is that effects which themselves are fleeting data are produced in my mind through the instrumentality of my body. But the faculty of the understanding now intervenes,[7] combining time and space, and adding such categories as substance, causality and existence. The outcome — the joint product of effects, time, space and categories — is not just a set of fleeting data in time, but a table — an object perduring in space and causally interacting with other objects. It is this table, and everything of the kind, that is objective and *real*, not fleeting effects in my mind.[8]

Mental images

Schopenhauer interrupts the flow of his exposition at this point to discuss mental images, arguing that this is the place to consider them because, while they do not belong to the totality of experience — that is, while they are not objective, not real objects — they are none the less complete. To illustrate his point, my mental image of a dog possesses not only such formal properties as having shape and lasting for a certain period of time, but such material properties as appearing black and glossy.

How can I tell mental images from real objects? How can I know, for example, that what is before my consciousness at a given moment is a mental image of a dog and not a real dog? Schopenhauer's answer is as follows. When I am awake, my body is present to my consciousness 'uninterruptedly, while other objects are not, and normally I am able to contrast mental images, which are fleeting, with my body which is continuous and stable in my consciousness. It follows that in cases where mental images are particularly vivid and I cease to be conscious of my body, I recognise that they are images only when I become conscious of my body

77

again. When I am asleep and therefore not conscious of my body, I cannot tell my mental images — my dreams — from real objects. I only recognise them to have been images when I wake up.[9]

This proposal for distinguishing mental images from reality is not very convincing, for a reason familiar to us from Plato's *Theaetetus*.[10] If at any given moment I appeal to a supposed contrast between images and my body, this presupposes that I am justified in thinking that I am aware of my body. But whatever occurs in my waking states can be imitated in my dreams, so that at any moment I could merely be dreaming that I am conscious of my body. It is worth adding that it is surely untrue anyway that I am always aware of my body continuously when I am awake.[11]

The principle of sufficient reason of becoming

So far in this chapter, Schopenhauer has discussed the following things: the nature of the first class of objects, what he means by the 'real' world, the role of the body in the perception of objects, and the distinction between mental images and real objects. He turns at last to considering the form of the principle of sufficient reason that governs the first class of objects. It is, he says, the law of causality, and what he has in mind will best be understood by means of an example.[12] If a piece of wood catches fire, this new temporary state of the wood — that is, the actual occurrence of its igniting — follows upon and is the effect of its coming into contact with oxygen together with its reaching a particular level of temperature. These events or new states of things in the world together constitute the cause of the wood's catching fire.

What precise relation does a cause bear to its effect? It constitutes the set of necessary and sufficient conditions for its occurrence. Put differently and generally, cause and effect are related in accordance with the following regularity: given the occurrence of a change that we call an effect, the state of affairs that we call its cause *must* have preceded it, and given the state of affairs that we call a cause, the change that we call its effect *must* follow it. In addition, remarks Schopenhauer, the state of affairs named the cause is itself a change, and is therefore in turn the effect of a preceding state of affairs; and so on indefinitely. Further, properly speaking it is the entire complex of relevant antecedent conditions that constitutes the cause, even though in ordinary conversation we pick out the last condition to occur and refer to that as the cause.

It will be clear by now what Schopenhauer means by referring to the principle of causality as the principle of sufficient reason of *becoming*. He means that whenever a change of state, a becoming, occurs in a physical object or physical objects, there is always a preceding change of state or complex of states sufficient to bring it about.[13]

There are two points that Schopenhauer adds.[14] One, the law of causality applies to *states*, not to *things*: it is the temporary state of the oxygen, not the oxygen itself, that brings into being the state of the wood's burning — it does not bring into being the wood itself. Two, given that in respect of necessity and sufficiency there is no difference between cause and effect, each constituting necessary and sufficient conditions of the other, what distinguishes cause from effect is simply temporal precedence.

Kant on the a priori nature of the principle of causality

Like Kant, Schopenhauer holds that the principle of causality is known to us a priori and that it is both necessary and universal in its scope; but he believes that Kant's proof of this, as presented in the *Second Analogy*, is fallacious. Accordingly, he now sets out to show that this is' so and to provide an alternative proof.

There is much dispute concerning the force and even the nature of the proof put forward by Kant, and there is no room to examine it in detail here;[15] the best course is simply to present it as Schopenhauer himself understands it.

Kant's argument

Kant's argument, as understood by Schopenhauer, is as follows. The imagination synthesises the manifold, and in doing so gives rise to succession. But succession as such is indeterminate in respect of order — indeterminate, that is, in respect of what follows what. Order is only introduced when the understanding applies its concepts of cause and effect.[16] Further, before the introduction of order there exists neither a world of experience nor *a fortiori* the possibility of objectively valid judgments. The principle of causality therefore is the condition of the possibility of experience, and is given to us a priori.

It follows further that the order in which sequences of changes occur in the objective world is itself recognised as objective only through the category of causality. In other words, the objectivity of sequences of representations — their correspondence to sequences in real objects — is known solely through the law of causality. A proof of this is that sequences not governed by the law of causality are reversible, as may be illustrated by the fact that we can observe the parts of a house in any order that we care to. In other words, the order in which we observe the parts of a house is dependent upon our choice, not upon a sequence that is objective. By contrast, if we watch a ship going down a river, our subjective apprehensions in this case are based upon an objective sequence, and consequently what is occurring is a genuine 'event.'[17]

Schopenhauer's criticisms of Kant's proof

Schopenhauer has the following points to make against Kant. First, experience does not depend upon the faculty of understanding alone, but equally upon the faculty of sensibility.[18]

Second, there is no real difference between the cases of the house and the ship. The sequences involved in both are 'events,' and knowledge of these sequences is consequently objective and recognised to be such by the relevant observers. What happens in the case of the ship is that changes occur in its position relative to the river. What happens in the case of the house is that changes occur in the eye of the observer relative to parts of the house, the movements of the observer's eye being just as much events as the sailing of the ship. Further, both sequences of impressions are brought about in the minds of the respective observers in the same way: by the causal impact of external objects upon their bodies.

Third, it is not true that we discern objectivity of change only through the law of causality, since there are many non-causal sequences that we recognise as objective. For example, my going out of the house and the falling of a tile, or the series of notes in a piece of music. We distinguish objective from subjective representations very well, then, without having to appeal to knowledge of causal sequences. Kant is wrong.

Finally, representations do not succeed one another only as a result of choice or in accordance with a rule, as Kant seems to think. There is a third way. Many representations succeed one another with a necessity that is not rule-governed; as, for example, countless objects successively affecting my body merely in time. Schopenhauer's point here is this. If I feel spots of rain on my face and then hear the sound of a passing car, this sequence is not part of a causal regularity. On the other hand, both occurrences are necessary, since each follows with necessity upon preceding sets of sufficient conditions.[19]

Schopenhauer's first proof

Schopenhauer offers two proofs of the a priori and necessary nature of the principle of causality. The first, which he touches upon but briefly, rests upon what he believes to be our unshakeable certainty that experience everywhere conforms to causality: we supposedly find it impossible to conceive of cases that escape it. Further, the only way to explain such certainty is to assume that its origin lies not in experience but in the unalterable structure of our minds. But this is to assume at the same time that it is given to us a priori.

There is much to be said for this argument. Most of us find it unusually difficult to believe that there could be events without causes; in fact it would seem that we are born with a tendency to believe the contrary. If this is so, it makes perfectly good sense to say of this belief in the universality of causality that it is given to us a priori. On the other hand, we have no convincing grounds for supposing it to be incapable of modification. In fact, in the present century we have grown accustomed to the idea that certain events do not have causes.

In brief, it is reasonable to hypothesise that the law of causality is an a priori principle, but not that it is necessary, unalterable and exceptionless.[20]

Schopenhauer's second proof

Schopenhauer's second proof may be summarised as follows. While our bodies and their states are the only objects given to us *immediately*, our consciousness is not confined to these. We are aware of such things as tables and chairs. How then do we get from our immediate conscious states to awareness of the external world? Schopenhauer's answer is this. While it is true that we are immediately aware only of bodily sensations, our faculty of understanding, applying its categories, *infers that there are causes* of these sensations, locating them in space and seeing them as substances. The outcome is that we perceive the external world of material objects. From this it follows that the category of causality is a condition of all external experience, and is therefore given to us a priori. We cannot have acquired it from observing constant conjunctions in the world of experience, since without it there is no such thing as experience in the first place.

It must be added, thinks Schopenhauer, that the inference made by our understanding to the external world is not conceptual, conceptual thinking and inferring being confined to the domain of the faculty of reason. An example, adapted from one of Schopenhauer's own, may help to bring out what is at issue here. If I see a crystal ball in a shop window, I do not employ conceptual, propositional reasoning to conclude that what I see is a sphere. Even so, some sort of inference takes place. At any rate, there is a good case for saying that I infer that I am seeing a sphere from such things as variations of light and shade; without such variations I should probably think that I am looking at a flat disk. Schopenhauer's point is that something like this happens in all cases of perception: we are immediately presented with sets of bodily sensations, not with external objects, and we infer the existence of the latter as causes of those sensations.

There are many difficulties attaching to this account of our belief in the external world, the first of which is that our own bodies need to be inferred, just as much as other objects in the world. However, Schopenhauer acknowledges this; and if his story is suitably modified, it turns out to have considerable plausibility.[21] There is a substantial case for saying that we are immediately confronted with nothing but subjective data — immediate representations, Humean impressions, or whatever else we might want to call them — and that no form of propositional reasoning, deductive or inductive, can justify our inferring a world beyond them. None the less, we do believe in such a world, and it is not implausible to describe that belief as the result of immediate inference, inference made before and independently of conceptual reflection.

Whether or not the external world that we infer is a world that exists independently of our minds or is a construction of those minds, as Schopenhauer holds, is a matter that would require more discussion than there is room for here.[22]

Two points need to be added. If Schopenhauer's story of how we come to believe in the external world is plausible, it follows, for reasons previously looked at, that there are good grounds for holding that the category of causality is given to us a priori. But it does not follow, for reasons also previously looked at, that every event in the external world has a cause. In other words, Schopenhauer's second proof, like the first, provides good grounds for holding that the principle of causality is given to us a priori, but not for holding that it is necessary and exceptionless.

Causality and the subject

The principle of causality is correctly applied only to changes in *objects*, thinks Schopenhauer, and the attempted application of it to *subjects* produces two false doctrines. The first of these is *realism*, a doctrine that results from thinking of subjects as causally affected by objects independent of them. (Schopenhauer has in mind the realist doctrine that material objects exist independently of us and causally affect us, thereby making us aware of them.) The second false doctrine is *idealism*, a doctrine that results from thinking of the world of objects as causally produced by a subject or subjects. (Schopenhauer perhaps has Fichte in mind here.)

The time of change

The principle of sufficient reason applying to the first class of objects governs changes in material objects, and Schopenhauer now briefly discusses the problem of 'the time' of such changes or, more generally, of change. According to Plato, change takes place in 'the sudden;' according to Kant, by contrast, it occupies a period of time. Kant argues that there is a period of time between any two moments, and consequently between any two states occupying time and following upon each other. It is in this intervening period of time that change takes place.

Schopenhauer very plausibly disagrees with Kant on this, asserting that there is no period of time between moments. Instead, there are clear cut boundaries between moments, and time is continuous,[23] together with all phenomena occupying time, including states of things. It follows that there is no such thing as a time between states in which change takes place, so that change does not really exist at all: it is a mere concept employed for making comparisons between states — for saying such things as that state *a* occurs before state *b*, or that state *a* no longer exists.

Schopenhauer ends by asserting, again very plausibly, that the 'present' is rather like change, and no less strange: it is a pure dividing line between past and future, and therefore does not occupy time and does not exist.

The second class of objects and the second form of the principle of sufficient reason: chapter five

The objects of Schopenhauer's second class are concepts. These he considers to be general, indeterminate and abstract, by contrast with objects of the first class, which are particular, determinate and concrete. An example will help to bring out the differences. Let us suppose that we have a dog named Harold. Harold is particular: he is a unique dog, an object located at precise points in space and time. All of his properties are fully determinate: his coat is black and glossy to a precise degree, his tail has a precise length and shape, his legs number precisely four, his eyes precisely two, and so on. Thirdly, we see Harold, hear him and feel him. In short, he is a concrete particular, belonging to the first class of objects, and we recognise him as such. But we also know that he is a dog. Moreover, we know what a dog in general is, what any dog is; and this is what is meant by saying that we possess the concept of a dog. Needless to say, we possess many concepts.

By contrast with concrete particulars, concepts are not located at precise points in space and time, and their properties are not fully determinate: our concept of a dog, for example, is not fully determinate in respect of being black, glossy, four-legged, or anything else. Again, the process by which we acquire knowledge of concepts is not that of seeing, hearing or feeling. It is a process of abstraction. First we perceive many particular dogs; then, by abstracting from all properties that are not essential to them as dogs, we acquire the general idea of a dog, the concept of a dog.

There is a temptation to think of concepts as mental images, and Schopenhauer rightly insists that they are nothing of the sort. Concepts are general, images are particular. If, for example, we close our eyes and conjure up an image of a dog, this image will possess at least some fully determinate properties — being black perhaps or yellow, big or small, fat or thin. If what we conjure up does not possess a set of such fully determinate properties, then — whatever else it is — it is not an image.

All of this fairly represents Schopenhauer on the nature of concepts, and even if this or that point is subject to doubt, owing to the brevity of his explanations, what is not subject to doubt is that he thinks of concepts as *objects*. Indeed this is his central assertion: concepts make up the second class of objects. They are representations, he holds, things 'present' to our minds as fully as are tables and chairs; the only difference is that they are not particular.

This central tenet of Schopenhauer's has little to commend it. Contrary to what he assumes, our minds do not contain objects devoid of determinate properties, as should be clear from the fact that if we wish to know whether or not we have the concept of a dog, of causality, or of anything else, we do not begin by searching our minds for indeterminate objects. What is more, Schopenhauer's belief that concepts are formed by abstracting from certain properties of particulars suggests that they are objects 'in' this or that mind: that each mind contemplates its own. In other words, it seems to suggest that from a set of particulars I form an object that dwells in my mind, while from the same set you form an object, possibly very different, that dwells in yours. But this is untenable. When you and I talk about tables and chairs in general, about the advantages of democracy, or about anything else of the sort, we are not discussing objects that exist privately in our several minds. We are discussing the selfsame things — tables, democracy, or whatever else.

Given these and similar difficulties, it is simpler and more plausible to think of concepts not as objects of this or that kind, but as capacities: capacities to recognise or otherwise think about common properties or characteristics.[24] If I possess the concept of a table, for instance, I have the capacity to recognise the characteristics of a table when I see one, to think about buying one, and so on: I do not 'see before my mind's eye' a colourless, shapeless, intangible item, nor an item that in some fashion has four legs, two legs and no legs all at once.

Concepts, judgments and reason

Concepts, says Schopenhauer, are of no use by themselves. Their value lies in the fact that linked together in appropriate ways they constitute true judgments, and the value of true judgments lies in the fact that these make possible such things as reasoning, syllogising and drawing conclusions. To illustrate the point, the concepts of man, animal and living organism have no value in themselves, but they can be used to form such true judgments as, 'All animals are living organisms,' 'All men are animals,' 'All men are living organisms;' and these judgments can be used for reasoning in the following way and similar ways:

All animals are living organisms.
All men are animals.
Therefore, all men are living organisms.

Schopenhauer's doctrine that judgments are concepts linked together in appropriate ways and expressed in language faces many difficulties, the most important of which concerns the nature of concepts. The difficulty here is this. If it turns out, for reasons outlined above, that concepts are not objects of this or that kind, but capacities, it is difficult to see how they can combine to form judgments — difficult to see, for example, how a number of mental capacities can combine to form the judgment, 'All men are mortal.' An effort might be made to avoid this difficulty by rather generously taking Schopenhauer to mean that concepts are universals or characteristics — thus explaining their generality — and that sentences therefore express and perhaps refer to combinations of universals. However, while this may do at a pinch for sentences like, 'All men are mortal,' it will not do for sentences like, 'Harold is a labrador.' For, to construe 'Harold' as referring to a set of universals leaves out of account how 'Harold' refers to our particular dog, as plainly it does.

Schopenhauer makes the intriguing suggestion, unfortunately not developed, that proper names do not refer to concepts, and that consequently they do not really belong to language. It is difficult to be sure what he means by this, but there is some plausibility in interpreting him to mean the following. In the sentence, 'Harold is a labrador,' to pursue that example, 'Harold' has no meaning — unlike 'labrador.' It has an exclusively referring function: it refers to Harold. If to this is added the doctrine that only signs possessing meaning belong to language, pure referring terms being excluded, it follows that 'Harold' does not belong to language at all. If this is what Schopenhauer means, his suggestion is undoubtedly a useful one.

However, there can be no value in saying more on the issue, or on concepts, judgments and meanings in general. What Schopenhauer says is too meagre to sustain more prolonged discussion.

Concepts, judgments and the principle of sufficient reason

How does the principle of sufficient reason apply to the second class of objects, to concepts? It applies, thinks Schopenhauer, indirectly and in the following way. Concepts are useful as the building blocks of judgments, but judgments are useful only in so far as they are true. What really matters then is not concepts or judgments as such, but true judgments.

What is a true judgment? Schopenhauer's answer is that a true judgment is one that is related to a reason or ground outside it that is sufficient for its truth. This of course does not tell us what being 'true' means, but it does make the following two points, which, if correct, are important. Every true judgment has a sufficient reason for its being true, just as every change has a sufficient reason for its occurrence. Second, the reason constituting the sufficient grounds for the truth of a judgment is in all cases external to the judgment itself: truth is never an intrinsic, nonrelational property.

It would perhaps have been better had Schopenhauer called this form of the principle of sufficient reason the principle of sufficient reason of *truth*. But he does not: he calls it the principle of sufficient reason of *knowing*. He does this because he considers that to know is one and the same thing as to be in possession of true judgments, so that what constitutes the sufficient reason for the truth of a judgment at the same time constitutes the sufficient reason for an instance of knowing. He also believes, as he explains in detail later on, that the principle of sufficient reason is a tool for acquiring systematic knowledge. Possibly he even has at the back of his mind that knowledge of truth is more important than truth considered in itself, and that consequently it is more proper to call the principle the principle of *knowing* than of *truth.*

Four kinds of truth

Schopenhauer believes that there are four and only four kinds of reason that can make a judgment true, and that consequently there are what may be called four kinds of truth.

First, the truth of a judgment may rest upon the truth of another judgment. What this means is that the truth of the judgment, say, 'Some men are mortal,' may be said to rest upon the truth of the judgment, 'All men are mortal.' That is, the truth of the judgment, 'All men are mortal,' is sufficient for the truth of the judgment, 'Some men are mortal.'[25] In cases of this kind, the judgment whose truth rests upon that of the other is said to have *logical* or *formal* truth. Schopenhauer adds, with much plausibility, that even judgments which at first sight appear to have intrinsic or non-relational truth are in fact 'logically' true. To illustrate his point, the truth of the judgment, 'No body is without extension,' may at first sight appear to be intrinsically or non-relationally true, but on reflection its truth will be seen to rest upon the principle of contradiction; that principle will be seen to provide sufficient reason for its truth.

Second, the truth of some judgments rests directly upon experience. What this means is that the truth of some judgments can be backed up by appeals to direct experience, and that they correspond to what the world of experience contains. If, for example, the cat is sitting on the mat, the judgment, 'The cat is on the mat,' can be backed up by an appeal to experience, precisely because the cat is sitting on the mat and may be seen to be doing so. In cases of this kind, judgments are said to have *empirical* truth.

Third, the truth of some judgments rests upon the conditions of all experience. To take an example, according to Schopenhauer the world of 'experience' — the public world of tables and chairs — exists only because it is subject to the principle of causality. If *per impossibile* it ceased to be made up of causally interrelated objects, it would cease to be a world of experience. And it is this fact that makes the judgment, 'Nothing happens without a cause,' true. This may be put rather differently in the following way. We do have a world of experience; that is an unquestionable fact. But we would not have such a world if what we are presented with were not governed by causality. That also is a fact, and it is this second fact that constitutes a sufficient reason for the truth of the judgment, 'Nothing happens without a cause.' More briefly, if there is a world of experience, as there is, the judgment has to be true that nothing happens without a cause. This kind of truth, resting upon the conditions of experience, is called *metaphysical.*

Fourth and last, the truth of some judgments rests, not upon the conditions of experience, upon our having a world of tables and chairs, but upon the conditions of our being able to think in any way at all. There are only four judgments of this kind: the principles of identity, contradiction, excluded middle, and sufficient reason of knowing. Once again the implicit argument is something like this: if these principles did not hold, we should not be able to think; therefore, the very fact that we can and do think constitutes sufficient grounds for their being true. Schopenhauer calls such truths *metalogical*.

It is worth noting in passing that a judgment can have more than one kind of truth. For example, the judgment, 'Some men are mortal,' may be said to have logical truth because the truth of the judgment, 'All men are mortal,' is sufficient for its truth. But it also has empirical truth. The judgment, 'Some men are mortal,' is true because as a matter of empirical fact some men are mortal.

Everything that Schopenhauer says about the second class of objects is sketchy, and many of his assertions are open to question. For example, it is open to question that the principle of causality in the exceptionless form intended by Schopenhauer is required for us to have a world of 'experience,' and it is equally open to question that exceptionless forms of the principles of excluded middle, identity and contradiction are necessary conditions of our being able to think. None the less, Schopenhauer's two main assertions are very probably true and, if so, important. The first of these is that there is a fundamental distinction between the particular and the general, however we may wish to account for it. Schopenhauer's way is to place concrete particulars in a sharply different class from concepts. The second is that the property of being true is a relational property: to say that a sentence or statement is true is to imply that it is related to a ground or reason external to it.

The third class of objects and the third form of the principle of sufficient reason: chapter six

The third class of objects has only two members: space and time. Following Kant, Schopenhauer holds that these are respectively the forms of our faculties of outer and inner sensibility: that is, to put the point more generally, space and time are the products of our minds and are imposed upon the way in which we view the phenomenal world of everyday experience.

Schopenhauer further holds, also with Kant, that space and time are 'pure perceptions a priori.' What he means by this is that space and time are not concepts, not abstractions from the world of experience, but particulars. That is, space and time are not concepts, like red, round, and so on, each having indefinite numbers of instances. There is and can be only one space and one time, and these are particulars in which are located such empirical items as tables, chairs and events. But space and time are not themselves empirical items, perceived through the bodily senses; rather, they are directly intuited by the mind. Moreover, the mind's intuition of them is obviously a priori, given that they are not known as a result of experience. Indeed without them there would be no such thing as experience in the first place; they themselves are major constituents of experience.

The structure of space and time

Time is made up of an infinite number of parts, called moments, all of which are precisely interrelated: each has its position in relation to and dependent upon the rest, rather like points on a line. Space too has an infinite number of parts, called points, lines, areas and volumes, and these again are so interrelated that the position of each is related to and dependent upon the positions of the rest.

Perhaps the simplest way to grasp how Schopenhauer views the nature of space is to think of it as comprising an infinite number of points, rather like marbles in a box, so tightly packed that there are no gaps between them; and to think of lines, areas and volumes as constituting subsets of these points. Given this model, it is obvious that the position of any one point or set of points depends upon the position of every other, and that if we know where the other points are located we know *eo ipso* where the first is. Further, if with this model in mind we focus our attention upon a selected set of points that together make up a triangle, we see at once that the position of each side of this triangle is related to and dependent upon the positions of its other sides, and that the magnitude of the angles and the area of the triangle, together with its other internal properties, are related to and dependent upon the positions and other properties of its sides.

Schopenhauer's fundamental teaching on the nature of space — and *mutatis mutandis* time — should now be clear. It is that each and every part of space, each and every point, line, area and volume, *is* where it is and as it is only because the other parts of space are where they are and as they are. To put the point differently, the position and the related properties of all parts of space constitute a sufficient reason for the positions and related properties of all other parts of space. Moreover, as was made clear earlier on, the reason in question is not causal, nor is it conceptual: it is a reason of being. It follows that we can ask of any spatial or geometrical property why it is as it is, and in principle receive an answer in terms of other spatial or geometrical properties. To revert to the example used before, we can ask why the angles of a triangle are as they are, and receive the answer that they are as they are because the sides of the triangle are as *they* are.

A supposed universal flaw in Euclid's proofs

Just as every part of space is conditioned by other parts of space, so every moment of time is conditioned by other moments of time, and Schopenhauer believes, again with Kant, that this provides the basis of arithmetic. He thinks of arithmetic as being at bottom a matter of counting, which can only take place over moments in time. This is a particularly unconvincing theory of arithmetic, and Schopenhauer does nothing to defend or even explain it; he assumes that Kant's teaching on it is right and that his readers are familiar with that teaching.

He has rather more to say about geometry. His general position on this has already been outlined, but something needs to be said of his views on Euclid and other geometers, and on how they seek to prove their theorems. They provide us, he says, with purely conceptual demonstrations, which leave us dissatisfied. Why? Because our natural desire is to *see* the relations that hold between the parts of space under consideration in this or that theorem, and proofs in geometry therefore should *show* us that the relevant geometrical relations are as their conclusions assert.[26]

It is hard not to feel some initial sympathy with Schopenhauer on this point, since one of the attractive features of following a theorem through in geometry lies in the feeling that we can in the end *see* the spatial relations in question for ourselves. None the less, on several points his assertions are open to challenge. To start with, he seems to hold that however complex a set of geometrical relations is, it can in principle be understood or grasped non-conceptually. This is very doubtful, since surely there is a limit to what the human mind can take in without the aid of language and concepts; and Schopenhauer not surprisingly confines himself to giving us two examples, neither of which in the outcome is very convincing. Second, the whole notion of 'seeing' geometrical relations with something like the eye of the mind is misleading, as recent developments in geometry or geometries underscore. To illustrate the point, we may think that with the aid of suitable drawings we 'see' that the angles of a triangle add up to 180°. But Riemannian and other geometries force us to think again. Perhaps we are mis-seeing; perhaps the angles add up to slightly more or slightly less than 180°. There is no way of settling this matter by further visual or intellectual scrutiny, or by any kind of more precise measurement. Further, Schopenhauer assumes that Euclid's conclusions are both uniquely correct and uniquely descriptive of space. Few mathematicians share that view today. Third, there are good grounds for suspecting that Schopenhauer has got the nature of geometry exactly the wrong way round: that geometry is purely conceptual, even its axioms being implicit definitions; and that consequently there is nothing to be 'seen' in the first place. Admittedly there is not universal agreement on this, but it is a view held by many mathematicians and so constitutes a serious challenge to those who would defend Schopenhauer.

To conclude these brief remarks. Schopenhauer is almost certainly wrong in holding that space is a 'pure a priori perception,' uniquely and correctly described by Euclid and Euclideans. Further, even if he is not wrong in holding this, he is surely wrong in holding that conceptual demonstrations in geometry are useless, and that we ought non-conceptually to 'see' everything for ourselves.

The fourth class of objects and the fourth form of the principle of sufficient reason: chapter seven

The objects of Schopenhauer's fourth class are 'subjects of willing,' individual wills. These are objects of our inner sense and are therefore in time.

Why is it that the subject of *knowing* is not the immediate object of our inner sense, but only the subject of *willing*? In other words, when I look into myself, why do I apprehend myself not as a knower or as knowing, but only as a will or as willing? Schopenhauer answers this question, not very persuasively, in the following way. To begin with, the subject of knowing is the 'condition' of all objects, and therefore cannot itself become an object. To put this in different terms, if *per impossibile* the subject of knowing became the object of its own knowing, it would no longer be the subject of that knowing — having become its object. Secondly, it is not possible to have knowledge of knowledge, because all knowledge is of synthetic propositions, and the proposition, 'I know,' is not synthetic. What this seems to mean is something like the following. All knowledge is of facts, so that all propositions expressing knowledge must be informative, synthetic propositions. Consequently, if I had immediate knowledge of myself as knowing, the proposition expressing that knowledge, 'I know,' would be synthetic. But it is not. 'I know' is a purely analytic proposition, the notion expressed by the term 'know' being analytically contained in the notion expressed by the term 'I.'[27] We can if we like, says Schopenhauer, make the statement, 'I know,' but all that this amounts to is asserting that there are objects for me, and this in turn amounts to no more than saying the word 'I.' What Schopenhauer again has in mind is that subject and object are so complementary that to talk of one is virtually to talk of the other, a point that he reinforces by saying that to talk about the faculties of the subject is much the same as to talk about the different classes of representations that are objects for it. To take the faculty of reason as an example, what Schopenhauer means is that talk about the faculty of reason is inseparable from, and virtually the same as, talk about concepts and judgments.

The relation between subject and object

It will be clear by now that the most important fact about consciousness for Schopenhauer is that it irreducibly comprises subject and object, and that these are inseparable. Philosophers have often made the mistake, he says, of considering the two to be separate; as a result of this, some have fallen into the error of believing material objects, together with space and time, to exist independently of knowing subjects, others into the error of believing the same about universals. Subject and object, to repeat, are complementary, correlative, inseparable. They are none the less distinct, and however much we abstract from specific differences between them, they remain two. Even to ask why they exist, adds Schopenhauer, is to presuppose their distinctness as well as their existence. What he seems to mean by this is that to ask a question, to be a questioner, is one and the same as being a *subject* seeking a new *object* of knowledge.[28]

Finally, before turning to consider the nature of willing and action, Schopenhauer makes the point that while only the subject of willing is the immediate object of our inner sense, this subject of willing is identical with the subject of knowing. We cannot understand how this is so, he says, but we do know that it is so; and we know it directly.

How we know this directly, given that we are not directly aware of ourselves as knowers, Schopenhauer does not explain. He simply comments that the identity of the subject of knowing with the subject of willing is the most remarkable thing about reality — what he calls 'the miracle of miracles.'

The meaning of 'willing' and related terms

With an eye to analysing the concept of action, Schopenhauer explicitly or implicitly defines a number of terms related to 'willing,' remarking that 'willing' itself is indefinable: we all know what it is and we all know that it can cause actions, but we cannot say what its essence is.
Action or *acting* is the effect of willing when this becomes causal.
Desire is willing as long as it does not become causal. If and when it does, it is willing in the fullest sense of the term.
A decision is an act through which causality is imparted to a desire.

Empirical character is the general manner of a person's acting. (Sometimes Schopenhauer speaks of empirical character as if it is simply the usual manner or pattern of a person's acting; sometimes as if it is a sort of empirical self, underlying and accounting for the person's 'characteristic' behaviour.)

Intelligible character is the unaltering state of a subject of willing — 'a timeless universal act of willing.' (Given the various things that Schopenhauer says of it, intelligible character seems to be identical with the subject of willing at the noumenal level — outside of time, but manifested in time in the form of empirical character.)

A motive is a reason for an action.

Being able to act means that the external conditions are satisfied for willing a given action to become causal.

N. B. Character and subject of willing are really identical. More briefly, my character is my will.

Action and the principle of sufficient reason of acting

How actions arise, and what Schopenhauer means by the principle of sufficient reason of *acting*, or the principle of motivation, will best be brought out by an example. Let us suppose that a person called Mary is convinced that she ought to help those who are less fortunate than she, and that because of this she donates a thousand dollars to the Red Cross. What would Schopenhauer say of Mary's action?

The following. Like every person, Mary has a character, in virtue of which we are able to predict how she is likely to behave in various circumstances. In respect of its existence at a timeless level, this character is her ultimate self and is called *intelligible*. As manifested at the temporal level in observable behaviour it is called *empirical*.

When Mary donates the thousand dollars to the Red Cross, she does so because she has a *motive*, and this motive is her conviction that she ought to help those who are less fortunate than she. What this motive does is cause in her a *desire* to contribute a thousand dollars to the Red Cross, and this desire in turn prompts or occasions her character to manifest itself in a *decision* to donate the thousand dollars. Finally, this decision renders Mary's desire causally active — makes it an instance of *willing* in the strictest sense of the term — and so Mary actually donates the money. The sequence in brief is: motive; desire; decision brought about by character; willing; overt action.[29]

It is important to note that on this account of Mary's action, a point in which it differs from others, Mary's motive does not cause her to donate the money: it merely causes her to desire to donate it. More important, her desire does not cause her to make the donation, or even to decide to make it. Her desire is no more than the occasion for Mary's character to manifest itself in a decision. This may sound like verbal manoeuvring, since if Mary's desire occasions her character to manifest itself in a decision, what else can this mean but that in some sense or other it causes her character to cause a decision? However, Schopenhauer himself thinks that the part played by character is not causal, and an analogy that he gives in later editions of the *Fourfold Root* makes clear what he has in mind. A person's character, he there holds, is analogous to one of the forces of nature — for example, the force of gravity. This force cannot be

90

causally affected, since it itself never changes; nor, for the same reason, can it causally affect anything else, since causes themselves are changes of state in material things. None the less, the force of gravity plays an obvious role in change, since changes act as occasions for it to manifest itself in various ways. To illustrate the point, if a rock is positioned near the edge of a precipice and I give it a push, I provide the occasion for the force of gravity to manifest itself, which it does in the fall of the rock. The force of gravity is not a cause, thinks Schopenhauer, and similarly a person's character is not a cause; a person's character is simply that person's inner force manifesting itself in decisions according to circumstances. Further, just as the ways in which the force of gravity manifests itself are predictable, so are the ways in which a person's character manifests itself. Both are fixed, unalterable.[30]

There are obvious difficulties to this account of action, and in any event many readers will consider it to be just one more form of determinism. If my character is as unalterable as the force of gravity, in what sense can I be said to be free? However, Schopenhauer's account is not unattractive, particularly in its uncompromising insistence that an action is not simply an event following upon events taking place outside of me. My actions have their ultimate source in my intelligible character, and because of this there can be no doubt concerning who is responsible for my decisions and my actions: they are through and through my own.

Given all of this, what now is the principle of sufficient reason of *acting*, the law of motivation? It is that necessarily every action has a motive preceding it, and from the outline given above it will be obvious in what sense and why Schopenhauer holds this. It will also be clear what relation this form of the principle has to objects constituting the fourth class — individual wills or subjects of willing — since individual wills and characters are at bottom the same.

The following final comment is worth making, a comment this time that is critical of Schopenhauer. Given the analogy between a person's character and the forces of nature, there is little fundamental difference between the principle of causality and the principle of motivation, certainly not enough to warrant treating them as radically different forms of the principle of sufficient reason. For when a match bursts into flame, its being brought into contact with oxygen and its reaching the needed degree of temperature constitute an occasion for the relevant chemical forces to manifest themselves. But, analogously, if I strike a match, the motive that I had in doing so constituted an occasion for my character to manifest itself in a decision. If Schopenhauer is right, the law of homogeneity must surely take precedence over the law of specification here.[31]

The range of the will's influence

The will can exert a causal influence not only on the external world but upon the knowing self, thinks Schopenhauer, compelling it to conjure up mental images or to think upon any topic. Sometimes our judgments and mental images seem to occur independently of other processes of mind; but they do not in fact do so. The appearance of judgments and mental images is always to be explained by reference to motives, even when we do not notice what these motives are.

Having said this, Schopenhauer mentions memory as an example of the knowing subject's obedience to the will, but what he says about it is anything but persuasive. This is because he thinks of it as awareness of present images rather than awareness of the past; and because in addition he speaks of good memory rather than of memory as such.

Feelings and the like

Schopenhauer concludes his seventh chapter with remarks on 'feelings, emotions, passions and the like,' and his reason for bringing them in here is partly that he judges some of them to be acts of will, partly because he wants to make clear that feelings do not constitute an additional class of objects and so do not warrant an additional form of the principle of sufficient reason.

Schopenhauer's account of feelings is brief and amounts to little more than a proposal for the following classification. Certain feelings, such as pain, are simply bodily states, and so come under the principle of causality. Others, such as fear and hatred, are acts of will, and so come under the law of motivation. (The interesting argument given for saying that feelings of this kind are acts of will, by contrast with feelings like pain, is that we are required to control and even suppress them.) Other feelings again, of which only one example is given, hypochondria, are combinations of bodily states and acts of will.

Schopenhauer's final comment in this chapter takes the form of a protest against speaking of 'moral,' 'religious,' or 'aesthetic' feelings. Religious and aesthetic states of awareness, he asserts, are on an altogether higher plane, and are only called feelings by those who fail to distinguish what is highest and noblest in human nature from what is lowest and even bestial in it.

It would have been interesting to hear more on this, but Schopenhauer takes the matter no further. It is, he says, beyond the scope of his thesis.

Conclusions: chapter eight

The method of establishing forms of the principle of sufficient reason by first establishing classes of objects, says Schopenhauer, is not the only conceivable method: a start might have been made from the faculties of the mind or from areas of knowledge and reasoning. However, he believes that his approach constitutes a more thorough investigation of the principle of sufficient reason in general and demonstrates the fundamental unity of its kinds.

It is not clear that this is right. Schopenhauer's investigation would probably have been just as thorough had he started from the faculties of the mind or from established areas of knowledge and reasoning, since either of these would doubtless have led him to consider their objects and the principles governing them. None the less, his approach follows a good metaphysical instinct: beginning with objects and their related principles has attracted philosophers from the time of Thales onwards.

Some general points

Schopenhauer now makes a series of general points relating to conclusions arrived at in his thesis, but none of them adds substantially to what has gone before, and it is difficult at times to see why he singles them out as important.

The first of the points is that the order in which earlier chapters investigate the forms of the principle of sufficient reason is not the systematic order, but one adopted for the sake of exposition; the systematic order would have started with the principle of sufficient reason of being in time, and ended with the principle of sufficient reason of knowing. The second point is that reasons of becoming and acting always precede their consequents, whereas reasons of knowing and being — at any rate in geometry — do not. The third is that the different forms of the principle of sufficient reason support hypothetical judgments, subject like all hypothetical judgments to the usual rules that modus ponens and modus tollens are valid, while denying the antecedent and affirming the consequent are invalid.[32] The fourth is that every cause has an infinite series of other causes preceding it, that every geometrical figure is bounded by further figures indefinitely and in all directions, and that every moment of time is preceded by an indefinite number of other moments; by contrast, every series of judgments comes to an end in an empirical, metaphysical or metalogical truth, and every series of motives starts from one of the first two classes of objects. The fifth and last point is that each of the sciences makes particular use of one form of the principle of sufficient reason: pure mathematics the principle of sufficient reason of being, physics the principle of sufficient reason of becoming, and so on.

Imagination and reason

Before ending, Schopenhauer clarifies some remarks he made earlier on about human imagination and reason. It is a mistake, he argues, to think of imagination as producing poets and artists, or of reason as producing men of virtue and saintliness. For while imagination is a necessary condition of poetic and artistic genius, it is equally a condition of stupidity. *Pari passu*, reason is a condition of virtue, but also of villainy. He concludes by hinting that in a later treatise he will examine the true nature of the artist and the saint.

Two principal results

Schopenhauer ends his thesis by stating what he believes to be its two principal results. The first is to have established that the principle of sufficient reason is the general expression of four different principles. In the light of this, all philosophers making use of it, he urges, ought on each occasion to say which specific principle they are appealing to and which kind of reason. There are too many cases, he adds, where they fail to do this, either confusing the notions of reason and cause or employing the word 'reason' without specifying its sense. Even Kant is at fault here, speaking *inter alia* of the thing in itself as the *reason* of phenomenal reality.

The second principal result is to have established that the four specific forms of the principle of sufficient reason arise from a single characteristic of consciousness, made manifest in the faculties of sensibility, understanding and reason. However, the fact that they have this common source in no way justifies talk of a reason pure and simple. There is no such thing, says Schopenhauer, any more than there is a triangle pure and simple.

Notes

1 In later editions Schopenhauer fills out his arguments against Descartes and Spinoza a little, but they are unsatisfactory, and neither Descartes nor Spinoza would have had difficulty in meeting them. See F. C. White, *On Schopenhauer's Fourfold Root of the Principle of Sufficient Reason*, Brill, Leiden and New York 1993, pp. 20-24.

2 In the 1847 edition Schopenhauer's approach is different but still not satisfactory. See F. C. White, op. cit., pp. 25f.

3 Concepts, that is, as Schopenhauer conceives of them — mental objects.

4 This point will become clear later on. As has been mentioned, Schopenhauer asserts that motives are not causes of actions, but the account of action that he proposes in his Chapter 7 is none the less causal in all but name — however unusual the kind of causality. An action is not caused by its motive, he says, but it *arises from* the empirical character (aus . . . erfolgt) when this is *prompted* (sollicitirten) by a motive (pp. 122f). Possibly Schopenhauer himself comes to acknowledge this; for, while his fundamental view does not change, in the 1847 edition of the *Fourfold Root*, §20, he says that a person's 'actions ensue with the same necessity as the rolling of a ball after it has been struck.' (. . . sein Thun mit eben der Nothwendigkeit erfolgt, wie das Rollen der gestoßenen Kugel). (See below, under *Action and the Principle of Sufficient Reason of Action*.)

5 In later years Schopenhauer is to claim that he has succeeded in reducing the twelve categories to one, namely causality. See, e.g., *Fourfold Root*, ed. 1847, p. 111.

6 My understanding of Schopenhauer's point is speculative; his argument contains too little detail to allow of more confident interpretation.

7 Not at some particular stage in time, of course. Schopenhauer (despite his mode of speaking here and there) is concerned with what we might call a metaphysical, not a temporal analysis.

8 There are of course difficulties facing this account of perception. See F. C. White, op. cit., Chapter 4, passim.

9 The only other way of telling images from reality, says Schopenhauer, is to find out if the body could have undergone the effect whose representation is included in the mental image. But this is very difficult, he adds.

10 *Theaet.* 157e-158d.

11 It is worth adding that real objects and their states also contrast with my body, but this does not show them to be mere mental images.

12 What Schopenhauer 'has in mind' may seem fairly commonplace

now, but it was not in his time, and he himself often slips back into talking of things rather than states as causes.

13 To talk of the principle of sufficient reason of becoming is to focus attention on causes as sufficient conditions for their effects — ignoring the fact that they are also necessary.

14 The second is clearly made (§23 ad fin.) but not fully stated.

15 On my reading of the *Second Analogy*, Kant makes the following assertions, all of which are open to serious challenge: 1) causal laws are necessary and universal in their application (an assertion made also by Schopenhauer); 2) all objective sequences (*a* followed by *b*) are causal; 3) all causal sequences are objective; 4) subjective sequences are not causal; 5) we recognise objective sequences as objective only by recognising that they are causal. I believe that Schopenhauer's criticisms of Kant are well justified.

16 Schopenhauer speaks of these as concepts, although elsewhere he makes plain that the category of cause as applied by the understanding is not a concept. See below, under *Schopenhauer's Second Proof*.

17 What Kant calls a *Begebenheit*.

18 It is a pity that Schopenhauer does not make more of this point, since the objectivity of experience is clearly as much to do with the public nature of space and time as it is to do with causality.

19 The necessity is conditional, not absolute.

20 *Pace* Kant and Schopenhauer himself, it does not follow from the fact that a proposition is a priori that it is necessary: the notion of a proposition's being a priori is epistemological, that of its being necessary is metaphysical.

21 In fact I believe it to be correct.

22 See F. C. White, op. cit., Chapter 4, passim.

23 The boundaries are clear cut in the sense of having no duration, thus ensuring that time is continuous.

24 See H. H. Price, *Thinking and Experience*, London 1956; and F. C. White, op. cit., Chapter 6, passim.

25 On the assumption that 'All men are mortal' has existential import.

26 Cf. Kant, *Critique of Pure Reason (CPR)*, II, Chapter 1, Section 1.

27 This is as little convincing as more recent attempts to argue that the proposition, 'I exist,' is analytic.

28 I assume that he does not mean, trivially, that in asking the question, 'Why do subject and object exist?' I presuppose that they exist, just as in asking, 'Why do Harold and Charis have the same mannerisms?' I presuppose that Harold and Charis exist.

29 No doubt Schopenhauer would allow that indirectly character also plays a part in accounting for motives and desires.

30 In later years Schopenhauer talks of the denial of the will in which character is totally suppressed. See *The World as Will and Representation* I, pp. 403f; II, pp. 609f.

31 Compare what Schopenhauer himself says in, e. g., *The Fourfold Root of the Principle of Sufficient Reason*, 1847 edition, pp. 212-214, and *The World as Will and Representation* I, p.102.

32 $[((p \Rightarrow q) \& p) \Rightarrow q]$ is valid; $[((p \Rightarrow q) \& \sim q) \Rightarrow \sim p]$ is valid; $[((p \Rightarrow q) \& \sim p) \Rightarrow \sim q]$ is invalid; $[((p \Rightarrow q) \& q) \Rightarrow p]$ is invalid.

Bibliography

Works by Schopenhauer

Ueber die vierfache Wurzel des Satzes vom zureichenden Grunde, Rudolstadt 1813.
Zürcher Ausgabe, Werke in zehn Bänden, Zürich 1977.
On the Basis of Morality, trans. Payne, E.F.J., Bobbs-Merrill: Indianapolis 1965.
Essay on the Freedom of the Will, trans. Kolenda, K., 2nd ed., Blackwell: Oxford 1985.
Parerga and Paralipomena: Short Philosophical Essays, 2 vols, trans. Payne, E.F.J., Clarendon Press: Oxford 1974.
On the Fourfold Root of the Principle of Sufficient Reason, 1847 ed., trans. Payne, E.F.J., Open Court: Illinois 1974.
On the Will in Nature, trans. Hillebrand, K., (revised ed.), George Bell: London 1903.
The World as Will and Idea, 3 vols, trans. Haldane, R.B. and Kemp J, Kegan Paul: London 1909.
The World as Will and Representation, 2 vols, trans.. Payne, E.F.J., Dover: New York 1969.

Works on Schopenhauer

Atwell, J. (1990), *Schopenhauer: The Human Character*, Temple University Press: Philadelphia.
Atwell, J. (1995), *Schopenhauer on the Character of the World: The Metaphysics of Will*, University of California Press: Berkeley.
Copleston, F. (1946), *Arthur Schopenhauer: Philosopher of Pessimism*, Burns Oates & Washbourne: London.
Fox, M. (ed.) (1980), *Schopenhauer: His Philosophical Achievement*, Harvester Press: Brighton.
Gardiner, P. (1963), *Schopenhauer*, Penguin: Harmondsworth.
Hamlyn, D. (1980), *Schopenhauer*, Routledge & Kegan Paul: London.

Janaway, C. (1989), *Self and World in Schopenhauer's Philosophy*, Clarendon Press: Oxford.

Janaway, C. (1994), *Schopenhauer*, Oxford University Press: Oxford.

Magee, B. (1983), *The Philosophy of Schopenhauer*, Clarendon Press: Oxford.

Young, J. (1987), *Willing and Unwilling: A Study in the Philosophy of Arthur Schopenhauer*, Nijhoff: Dordrecht.

White, F.C. (1992), *On Schopenhauer's Fourfold Root of the Principle of Sufficient Reason*, Brill: Leiden.

Index

a priori necessity 71
ability to act 54
acting 54
actions
    and freedom 41
Aesop 57
animals
    character of 57
Apuleius 14
Aristotle 5-6, 10, 27
arithmetic 45

basic principles of thought 41-42
Baumgarten 8, 10
being
    see existence
body 77

categories 43
    and deduction 14
    and induction 14
    and table of judgments 40
category of unity 53
causality 22-32
cause
    and objects 22-23, 81
    par excellence 22
    Plato on 5
change 17
    time of 32-34
        Plato on 32-34
        Kant on 32-34, 82
character
    empirical 55-58, 90
    intelligible 55-58, 90

Christianity
    and temporality 68
coexistence 16-17
cognitive faculties
    knowledge of 51
coincidence 25
common root of reasons 13, 74-75
concepts 20, 82
    as objects 83
    judgments and reason 83-84
    nature of 36-37
    uses of 37
continuity 34
criterion 31

decisions 54, 55-58
    and time 55
Democritus 34
Descartes 6, 67
desires 54, 55
dogmatic philosophers 52
dreams 20-22, 26
duration 16-17

ethics and aesthetics 56
Euclid 45-49
    proofs 87-88
    sixteenth theorem 48-49
    sixth theorem 46-47
existence
    or being
    absolute 18
    infinitive of verb 19
experience 24
    and causality 27

For Product Safety Concerns and Information please contact our EU
representative GPSR@taylorandfrancis.com Taylor & Francis Verlag GmbH,
Kaufingerstraße 24, 80331 München, Germany

Printed and bound by CPI Group (UK) Ltd, Croydon, CR0 4YY
11/04/2025
01843992-0009